My God,
Why?

Wallace T. Viets

My God, Why? And Other Questions from the Passion

ABINGDON PRESS
Nashville • New York

MY GOD, WHY?

Copyright © 1966 by Abingdon Press

Library of Congress Catalog Card Number: 66-10848

"But This Is Also Everlasting Life" is from *Portraits and Protests*
by Sarah N. Cleghorn. All rights reserved. Reprinted by permission of Holt, Rinehart and Winston, Inc. "Indifference" from
The Unutterable Beauty by G. A. Studdert-Kennedy. Reprinted by
permission of Harper & Row.

Manufactured in the United States of America

TO

MARIAN
WESLEY
ROBERT
and
RAYMOND

in hope that their consideration of these crucial questions and their search for the answers in their own lives will bring them closer to understanding God's purposes for them

Question and answer has long been recognized as an effective way of teaching and has been used from time immemorial. Discussion rather than dogmatic pronouncement seems a much more fruitful method of communication in our day. I have long felt that, if a sermon is to be effective, it will be, in effect, an adventure in co-operative thinking between the preacher and the congregation. I think this idea of the sermon comes originally from Harry Emerson Fosdick. At any rate, it has long been a guiding one for my own thinking and preaching. I have tried for years to stimulate thinking from the pulpit with the rhetorical question and often leave the answers open-ended.

For these reasons the vast number of questions that dot the pages of Scripture have great fascination. This series of sermons based on questions has evolved through the years both in Lenten Bible study and in Lenten preaching.

I am grateful to many who cannot be listed, but would thank those who suggested that these be printed; those who have had some part in my education, particularly the late Halford E. Luccock and my parents and wife, whose constant loving support has not prevented them from giving helpfully critical guidance.

Ideas come from many sources. Careful attempt has been made to give credit wherever possible. Thanks are offered for them and also to those who transcribed the original tape recordings and helped in their editing.

This series of sermons was preached, in substantially its present form, from the pulpit of the First Methodist Church of New Haven, Connecticut, where the first six also served as a basis for Lenten prayer and study groups. The encouragement of members of the congregation is gratefully acknowledged.

WALLACE T. VIETS

CONTENT

Introduction 11

1. Is It I?
   THE PERSONAL QUESTION 13

2. Shall We Strike with the Sword?
   THE QUESTION OF FORCE 26

3. What Is Truth?
   THE ACADEMIC QUESTION 41

4. What Shall I Do with Jesus Who Is Called Christ?
   THE INESCAPABLE QUESTION 52

5. My God, Why?
   THE QUESTION FROM SUFFERING 66

6. Who Is This?
   THE QUESTION FROM THE WORLD 78

7. Why Do You Seek the Living Among the Dead?
   THE QUESTION OF LIFE 87

Epilogue. Do You Love Me More Than These?
   THE CONTINUING QUESTION 99

Notes 111

Introduction

Liberally scattered throughout the Gospel accounts are questions asked by and about Jesus Christ. Many of these appear in the passion narratives. Together they raise important issues not only for the passion narratives themselves, but also for our continuing understanding.

In the collection of questions which has served as a basis not only for a series of Lenten sermons (including, as an epilogue, one for the Sunday after Easter) but also as a basis for prayer and study group sessions, we find two questions asked by Jesus; two by the disciples; two by Pilate; one by curious bystanders; and one by an angel.

If it is desired to use these sermons also as a basis for Bible study, the parallel passages (in addition to the scriptural passages printed at the head of each sermon) will be found useful. These are as follows:

1.—Matthew 26:17-30; Luke 22:7-30 and John 13:21-30
2.—Matthew 26:47-56; Mark 14:43-52 and John 18:1-12
3.—Matthew 27:11-14; Mark 15:2-5 and Luke 23:2-3
4.—Mark 15:6-20; Luke 23:13-25 and John 18:39-19:16
5.—Matthew 27:32-56; Luke 23:26-49 and John 19:16-37

6.—Mark 11:1-11; Luke 19:29-44 and John 12:12-19

7.—Matthew 27:57–28:10; Mark 15:42–16:8 and John 19:38–20:18

Epilogue—compare versions of the Great Commission in Matthew 28:16-20; Mark 16:14-18 (and the alternative verse printed as a footnote in the RSV) and Acts 1:6-8.

1. "Is It I?"

THE PERSONAL QUESTION

(First Sunday in Lent)
Scripture: Mark 14:12-26

Stretch your imagination for a moment and try to think what it was like to be a member of a wandering band, traveling around the countryside with a beloved teacher. Imagine that you had spent from one to three years, on terms of great intimacy, with this leader and his other followers. In him you saw not only a great teacher but the hope of deliverance for your subject nation. You saw one with great compassion for the multitude.

You and the others in the band are gathered with him to celebrate the preparation for a celebration which is both religious and patriotic. You are sharing bread with him around a table. In the course of the table conversation he states simply and with little emotion, except perhaps, deep sorrow, "One of you will betray me." What would your reaction be?

Consider this expansion of the simple declarative statement: One of you who has been so close to me; one of

13

you who has dipped his hand into the ceremonial bowl, as well as into the common larder from which we have eaten together; one of you who has shared all the intimacy of this difficult life—one of you will betray me. How would you have responded?

Review for a moment the events of the previous week leading up to this. There was the triumphal entry into the city, with the people hailing him, spreading their cloaks and palm branches and singing their praises, or shouting, "Hosanna!" There was the cleansing of the temple the next day as he struck that great blow for freedom of the exploited, or so it seemed at the time. Then there was the day of discussion and search for understanding and truth followed by a day of retirement and intimate fellowship in preparation for the climax. Now Jesus and the others have come together in preparation for the Passover. Undoubtedly a feeling of close fellowship existed in that upper room. This closeness was shattered by the words, "One of you will betray me."

I

Consider now the scene. As I read the Scriptures, more and more I become convinced that the intonation in the voice of Jesus when things like this are said, is not one of condemnation, nor even of anger. Rather, the tone seems to be one of disappointment perhaps, but, more particularly, of sorrow.

Note the initial reaction of the disciples. If we are honest with ourselves, I think we will admit that our first reaction to the announcement of impending betrayal would be,

14

"It's not I!" "I'd never do a thing like that!" But this is *not* the first reaction of the disciples as described in all four of the Gospel accounts.

If we continue to be honest with ourselves, I can imagine our second reaction to the announcement might well have been, "I wonder which of these other fellows is going to do this awful thing? I've wondered a little bit about him for quite a while! That other one isn't too dependable, either." Jesus is sorrowful at the breaking of the companionship in the group.

Phillips Brooks pointed out the maturity of the disciples in their reactions. Each one responds by saying, "Could it be I?" Unlike so many of us, each disciple seems to recognize in himself, at the same time he has a vision of greatness come to earth through this Messiah, this Christ—each recognizes in himself great possibility for evil as well as for good. Each recognizes weakness in himself. He sees that maybe he is not quite what he ought to be or might become. "Is it I?" Each asks the question.

Incidentally, in three of the four accounts, Judas is not specifically designated as the one who will betray. There is some question about the nature of the designation in the fourth one. He may have been singled out with some other purpose in mind. Furthermore, it seems very strange, if Judas had been singled out as the betrayer, that nothing was done by the others to restrain him. This all lends support to the idea that Judas was not specifically identified as the betrayer. Whether Jesus knew it or not is unimportant. "One of you will betray me." "Is it I?"

The universal condemnation of Judas in retrospect may

15

well be an unconscious device on the part of the rest of us to make ourselves appear not quite so bad! We are often like those of whom Samuel Butler wrote so wisely, who

> Compound for sins they are inclined to
> By damning those they have no mind to.[1]

At any rate, stages of moral growth are reflected by the possible reactions already suggested and the actual reaction as recorded. First, there is the proud confidence of the individual who immediately insists, "It couldn't be I." There follows the suspicious thought, "Which of these others?" Then comes the humble maturity of "Could it be I?" Whether fully recognized or not, the disciples expressed the possibility of great evil as well as of great good in each individual.

II

It may well be the disciples recognized that, in a very real way, they had already betrayed Jesus. We read in the Scripture that even in the conversation in the upper room the disciples were arguing with one another about who was to be most important in the new kingdom! They were jockeying for personal power and position. Is this not a betrayal of the fundamental ideas that Jesus had tried to implant in their minds? *He* said, "I am among you as one who serves."

In a scene recorded in the Gospel account Jesus and the disciples were traveling down from the north through Samaria toward Jerusalem and passed a village. The Samaritans were not too friendly, and in this particular vil-

16

lage they were most inhospitable. James and John came to Jesus and said, in effect, 'Lord, don't let them get away with this! Call down fire from heaven and wipe these people out!" (Luke 9:52-55.) James and John had betrayed him in this, had they not?

On another occasion we are told that many flocked around Jesus and brought children to him, but the disciples tried to drive the parents and children away. (Matt. 19:13-14.) Or again, Philip in the upper room is recorded in the Fourth Gospel as asking Jesus to show them the Father in order that they might believe. Jesus is surprised at their blindness. Are not these instances of a type of betrayal in refusing to see his message?

Then, you will remember, Peter, after the wonderful experience on the Mount of Transfiguration, not only tried to get Jesus to stay up on the mountain, but later, when he learned that Jesus was planning to go to Jerusalem, tried to dissuade him because it was too dangerous. Then there come those strange words as Jesus says to Peter, "Get thee behind me, Satan! You are a hindrance to me; for you are not on the side of God, but of men." (Matt. 16:23.)

Yes, perhaps the disciples were all too conscious of the fact that they had betrayed him before. Maybe there was dawning consciousness in the midst of their confusion that they had betrayed him by trying to make him what they wanted instead of letting him make them what he needed.

III

What about us? We have broken bread with him, symbolically. We have known intimate fellowship with him.

17

Have we made the gospel irrelevant in the day in which we find ourselves? Have we, as E. Stanley Jones has suggested, innoculated the world with a mild form of Christianity so that it is now practically immune to the real thing? It has been suggested that our churches are made up of people who would be equally shocked to see Christianity doubted or put into practice!

Have we made the gospel irrelevant by saying the church should mind its own affairs and if people are starving, lest we be accused of tampering with the sacred economic process, let them starve! Do we say that even though people may be indiscriminately destroyed through the imbecility and idiocy as well as the fundamental irreverence of war, then let them be destroyed, but keep the church out of politics! "One of you will betray me." "Is it I?" Have we betrayed him by making the church irrelevant to the world in which we live?

Dorothy L. Sayers is chiefly famous for her detective stories. She also has great interest in theology. In the Introduction to her play entitled *The Man Born to Be King* she writes in part:

Not Herod, not Caiaphas, not Pilate, not Judas ever contrived to fasten upon Jesus Christ the reproach of insipidity; that final indignity was left for pious hands to inflict. To make of His story something that could neither startle, nor shock, nor terrify, nor excite, nor inspire a living soul is to crucify the Son of God afresh and put Him to an open shame. . . . Let me tell you, good Christian people, an honest writer would be ashamed to treat a nursery tale as you have treated the greatest drama in history.[*]

18

"One of you will betray me." Have we done it by making the greatest story of all time insipid?

Some years ago, Halford Luccock in his column "Simeon Stylites" in *The Christian Century* had an essay entitled "Like a Mighty Army." It went something like this: The rector of St. John's-by-the-Gas-Station asked a member of his congregation to speak on Laymen's Sunday. The speaker was a returned serviceman. He requested that before his sermon the congregation should sing "Onward Christian Soldiers." The column goes on:

This is what he said: 'You have been singing
> Like a mighty army
> Moves the church of God.

That might have been all right once. The trouble is now that just about ten million men know exactly how an army moves. And it doesn't move the way a lot of you folks at St. John's do— or do not. Suppose the army accepted the lame excuses that many of you people think are good enough to serve as an alibi for not attending Church Parade.

"Imagine this, if you can. Reveille seven a.m. Squads on the parade ground. The sergeant barks out, 'Count fours.' 'One!' 'Two!' 'Three!' Number Four missing. 'Where's Private Smith?'

"'Oh,' pipes up a chap by the vacant place, 'Mr. Smith was too sleepy to get up this morning. He was out late last night and needed the sleep. He said to tell you that he would be with you in spirit.'

"'That's fine,' says the sergeant. 'Remember me to him.'

"'Where's Brown?' asks the sergeant.

"'Oh,' puts in another chap, 'he's out playing golf. He gets only one day a week for recreation, and you know how important that is.'

" 'Sure, sure,' is the sergeant's cheerful answer. 'Hope he has a good game. Where's Robinson?'

" 'Robinson,' explains a buddy, 'is sorry not to greet you in person. But he is entertaining guests today and of course couldn't come. Besides, he was at drill last week.'

" 'Thank you,' says the sergeant, smiling. 'Tell him he is welcome any time he is able to drop in.'

"Honest, now, did any conversation like that ever happen in any army? Don't make me laugh. If any G.I. tried to pull that stuff he would get twenty days in the guardhouse. Yet you hear stuff like that every week in the church, and said with a straight face, too.

"Like a mighty army! Why, if St. John's really moved like a mighty army, a lot of you folks would be court-martialed!" [3]

"One of you will betray me." "Is it I?"

We also sing about the church, "One in hope and doctrine, one in charity." Have we, after two thousand years, yet learned to disagree honestly and on the basis of conviction, but within the framework of charity and mutual respect? Have we learned to love despite our differences? It is easy to become discouraged when one hears people railing against the nations for being unable to resolve their differences and these same people cannot themselves meet within the Christian fellowship with a brother who holds a different social or political point of view. If Christians cannot agree to disagree and resolve to love and out of different interpretations and different understanding grow together closer to the stature of the fullness of God in Christ, then what hope is there for the world? "One of you will betray me." "Is it I?"

Have we tried to remake the gospel into our own image? George Bernard Shaw in his play *Saint Joan* has a scene that has long stuck in my memory. It is the sixth scene in the play. The English Bishop of Beauvais, the Roman Inquisitor, an English Chaplain and an associate, are drawing up the Bill of Particulars on which Joan is to be tried. They have a list of sixty-four charges. The Inquisitor has reduced them to twelve. The Chaplain objects. In the course of the ensuing discussion, this following dialogue takes place:

Chaplain: The Maid has actually declared that the blessed saints Margaret and Catherine, and the holy Archangel Michael, spoke to her in French. That is a vital point.
Inquisitor: You think, doubtless, that they should have spoken in Latin?
The Bishop: No; he thinks they should have spoken in English.
Chaplain: Naturally, my lord.

We enjoy the picture of Sallman's head of Christ. But Jesus didn't look like that. Jesus was not of Teutonic stock as is that figure in the picture. There may be validity in seeing the Incarnation in terms of every group, but not exclusively. Look at Daniel Fleming's *Each With His Own Brush*,[4] and see great spiritual insight as each group has represented Christ in terms of his own racial characteristics and then realize that the Incarnation cannot be confined to one group. Have we tended to put him into our own mold and pass judgment upon him in terms of what we accept?

It is a major triumph for the devil, writes Stringfellow Barr, that he has persuaded so many Americans

21

that the only source of sin is Communism. Being persuaded, they will not think to examine their own hearts. The Kremlin becomes hell, [Khrushchev] becomes Lucifer, Communist officials become demons, anti-Communists become the saved and ex-Communists, those most precious souls, the repented sinners. All sins except Communism pale to nothingness or are venial. We can gladly overlook roguery or malfeasance in high office, provided the rogue is fighting Communism. Thus sin seems to be disposed of and, being but *human,* we sigh with relief.[5]

"One of you will betray me." "Is it I?"

Every person whose name is now on the rolls of a Methodist Church once, in a solemn moment, stood before the altar of a church and took four vows. Members of other denominations took similar vows. These are the Methodist ones: "Will you be loyal to The Methodist Church, and uphold it by your prayers, your presence, your gifts, and your service?" Now, no one forced any other person to take these vows. No one held a club over his head and insisted. The vows were taken freely. Have they been kept? "One of you will betray me." "Is it I?"

IV

Up to this point we have painted a very somber picture. We can assume there was great consternation in the upper room when Jesus made his announcement. However, if we take the memories of all four of the evangelists and put their accounts together, we discover that this was not the end of the conversation in the upper room. Jesus said some other amazing things, too.

22

In order to experience pardon that leads to power, one must go through penitence. The person who is convinced that there is nothing lacking and that he needs nothing can receive nothing. Lent is a period when we move from the need for penitence, to the expression of that penitence and then through pardon to power. This is foreshadowed in the upper room conversation. In addition to the discovery of the disciples of the infinite possibilities for evil in each person, Jesus pointed out the infinite possibilities for good as well! Hear these words: "You did not choose me, but I chose you and appointed you that you should go and bear fruit and that your fruit should abide." (John 15:16.) Later he makes the incredible statement which would be blasphemous from any lips but his: "He who believes in me will also do the works that I do; and greater works than these will he do." (John 14:12.)[6] He is saying to each of them (and to us), "You will render great service!" To which we can but reply, "Is it I?"

Peter on the Day of Pentecost stood up at risk of life and limb and preached a great sermon proclaiming the truth as he understood it and spent the rest of his life proclaiming it. Sometimes he stumbled and groped, trying to understand, but never flinching from the proclamation. He gave his life on a cross outside Rome.

James, who had suggested calling down fire from heaven to destroy the Samaritan village, became the first of the twelve to give his life for his faith. Thomas, who refused to accept anything on faith, traveled, according to ancient tradition, to India and established a church which persists to the present day. Philip, who had been so blind in the upper room that he couldn't see what Jesus was driving at, we are told in Acts, went down to Ethiopia and Egypt and established the Coptic Church. "You will render great service." "Is it I?"

Call the roll of the "endless line of splendor" down through the centuries of those, who, fearful and uncertain at first, have rendered great service: Saul of Tarsus, Augustine of Hippo, Francis of Assisi, John Hus, John Wycliffe, Martin Luther, John Wesley, William Carey, Francis Asbury, Jesse Lee, Albert Schweitzer, Martin Luther King—the list is endless. Think of the unnumbered millions, unknown in the pages of history books, but, nevertheless, those of whom our Master could say, "Well done, good and faithful servant!" "You will render great service." "Is it I?"

V

But what of us?

There are many who make special arrangements for disciplined living during Lent. Here is a Lenten covenant that some have used:

All I am and have comes from God. Therefore, I promise him that I will conscientiously endeavor to be a faithful steward. In token of my gratitude, I promise during the Lenten season:

to engage in daily personal devotions, remembering the other members of the Christian fellowship in my prayers.

to worship regularly in the sanctuary on Sunday mornings.

to set aside ————% of my income for his greater glory and to maintain his kingdom.

24

to render certain additional services of which I will inform the pastor.

Signed _____

Why not try it? For Lent is not a period during which we would emphasize what we give up but is a period in which we seek that to which we shall give ourselves. Who knows? The Lenten experience might be such that it would carry over into the rest of the year as well!

"You will render great service." "Is it I?"

VI

After the conversation in the upper room and before going out to Gethsemane, Jesus prayed for his disciples and also for you and me, as part of his longer prayer for himself. In the course of the prayer he says,

I am praying for them . . . keep them in thy name . . . that they may be one, even as we are one. . . . I do not pray that thou shouldst take them out of the world, but that thou shouldst keep them from the evil one. . . . I do not pray for these only, but also for those who are to believe in me through their word. . . . The glory which thou hast given me I have given to them. (John 17:9, 11, 15, 20, 22.)

"One of you will betray me."
"Is it I?"
"You will render great service."
"Is it I?"

2. "Shall We Strike with the Sword?"

THE QUESTION OF FORCE

(Second Sunday in Lent)
Scripture: Luke 22:47-54

Of all the questions from the Passion, this one is, in many ways, the most difficult for us to consider objectively. The emotional atmosphere in which we have lived for nearly a full generation now is such that dispassionate analysis is almost impossible. That does not lessen, but rather, increases the importance of the question. In these days, even more than in some others, the church has the responsibility to lift up difficult questions, particularly on matters of life and death, in hopes that cooperative thinking, guided by the grace of God, may lead us toward solution. It is in this spirit, rather than with any feeling of dogmatic certainty, that the question of force is raised this morning. We dare not avoid it!

I know, personally, how difficult it is to consider this question dispassionately. Some years ago, in a former parish, I was preaching on this same text. I had reached the midpoint in the sermon when a middle-aged man, sitting on the center aisle, very ostentatiously took his coat from beside him, picked up his hat, and stood up. With a voice audible to everybody in the congregation, he said, "Boy, I can't take any more of this!" and turned and strode out. In over seven years that was the only time he ever did such a thing, and he was a very regular attender at our services. Yes, this is a most difficult subject.

However, we shall make the attempt to think helpfully about this which is a matter of life and death. "Lord, shall we strike with the sword?"

We shall attempt to reconstruct the scene and the sequel and then raise and consider four questions: Why do men use the sword (or any other weapon)? What does it accomplish? What effect does it have on the sword-wielder? What are the alternatives?

I

Reconstruct the scene.

Jesus had experienced the fellowship meal in the upper room and there had been talk about the new covenant. With his disciples he had gone from the upper room to the Garden of Gethsemane where he struggled with the temptation to run away. He submitted to God's will and, in so doing, received the strength to endure what had to be endured. Now, he and the three (then later, the other eight) were coming down off the rise of ground in the garden as Judas came in through the gate leading the temple guard. The crisis was approaching. In a moment would come a direct encounter between good and evil.

As they met, there was a sign of greeting, and Jesus was

27

seized. Did the disciples expect a miraculous deliverance at this point? At any rate, it did not come. One of the disciples whipped out a sword. Whatever his motivation may have been, his skill left a great deal to be desired! We are told he struck off the right ear of one of the servants of the high priest. If he was right-handed and struck off the right ear of someone who was facing him, his swordsmanship was awkward, to say the least!

Jesus responded to this action by saying, "No more of this! Put up your sword into its place; for all who take the sword will perish by the sword." Then he healed the ear and was led away.

The four Gospel accounts record this event a little differently. Only in Luke is the question, "Shall we strike with the sword?" actually asked, though in the other three accounts, swords are pulled out. Only in Matthew does Jesus give the unequivocal statement, "All who take the sword will perish by the sword." However, in the other three accounts, it is very clear that Jesus does not want them to use their weapons.

It can be said (and has been) that this was a unique situation and therefore cannot be generalized. But we can use it as an introduction to a consideration of the issue. For all the Gospel writers agree that in the conflict between good and evil (at least in this instance) swords were inappropriate. They were not used.

II

What was the sequel to this? What followed in the lives of Christians from the revelation of God's purpose brought

28

by Jesus Christ? For the first three centuries in the Christian church, it was felt that it was impossible for a Christian to be a soldier. We cannot evaluate that fact completely, but we cannot ignore it either. It was not until the time of Constantine that it was thought possible for a Christian to wield a sword.

Arnold J. Toynbee, in his book *War and Civilization* has written: "War has been proved to have been the proximate cause of the breakdown of every civilization which is known for certain to have broken down." [1]

Who of us is not aware of the atmosphere in which we find ourselves right now? Winston Churchill characterized it as a "balance of terror." One has suggested that the world today is like two men out of a Western movie, sitting across the table from each other, each with his six-gun drawn, cocked, and pointed at the heart of the other. Each knows that if he pulls the trigger, the involuntary reflex of his opponent in death will cause his trigger to be pulled and that both will die. So they sit, balanced on the edge of annihilation.

Have you read the current "horror" stories such as *Fail-Safe* by Eugene Burdick and Harvey Wheeler or *Triumph* by Philip Wylie or seen the movie *Dr. Strangelove*? Regardless of our attitude toward the details of the plot, it should be noted that Burdick and Wheeler are not pulp magazine writers but are college professors concerned to alert the nation to real danger. Philip Wiley's book deals with the experience of the eleven Americans who survived a nuclear holocaust in a deep bomb shelter. The mixture of horror and humor in *Dr. Strangelove* makes it hard to know whether to laugh or weep.

On February 15, 1963, MacGeorge Bundy, special assistant to the President of the United States, addressed alumni in the Yale Law School auditorium. Among other things, he said,

Our aim is to maintain a nuclear posture which makes it clear to all that nuclear war is not something anyone should want. We have succeeded for 17 years in this purpose, but the task is not made easier as time goes on. . . . There is a real chance that nuclear war may break out by some terrible mischance or malice.[2]

In a session on "Reactions to Nuclear War" [held in 1963] Harvard Medical School psychiatrist Lester Grinspoon observed that the public, and many decisionmakers as well, have not fully grasped the extent of the threat to civilization. . . . "The reason why it is not embraced," he argued, "is because it is not acceptable. People cannot risk being overwhelmed by the anxiety which might accompany a full . . . grasp of the present world situation."

All the classical mechanisms of psychological rejection are used to defend against the truth. One is simple denial of the facts; another is rationalization: "It's so terrible it'll never be used."[3]

There comes to mind a cartoon seen many years ago which showed two men standing before a dwelling. One was holding a weapon and he said to the other, "War has now become so horrible that men will find other ways of resolving their disputes." The dwelling before which they are standing is a cave and the weapon one of them is holding is a bow and arrow!

Dr. Grinspoon said he discerned a more modern defense mechanism at the higher levels of government which he called intellectualization. An expert's thorough grasp of the technical aspects of nuclear war "serves to keep him somehow quite distant from the psychological and political actualities. Doctors make frequent use of intellectualization; so do strategic thinkers." Dr. Grinspoon noted that these mechanisms are not only common, but may be essential to maintain normal existence. Even unrealistic optimism seems better than total and paralyzing fear.

But this misses the point, doesn't it? Regardless of what we may do with the textual criticism involved in an analysis of Matthew's "All who take the sword will perish by the sword," it certainly seems true in a world where "massive retaliation" and "over-kill" are current words, that all who take the bomb will perish by the bomb!

III

There are four basic questions that need to be considered. We are not going to answer them definitively, but perhaps we will point the direction toward answers.

First, why do men use the sword? Under what circumstances and for what reasons do men turn to weapons of destruction?

When the first atom bomb was dropped over Hiroshima, just about every Protestant minister in the country preached at least one sermon on the moral implications of the atom bomb. Perhaps I was derelict, but I did not preach such a sermon. I refrained because I felt there were no moral implications to the atom bomb which are not inherent in any other weapon. The difference is only in degree, not in kind—quantitative not qualitative.

But why do men use weapons which can cause death, whether individually or wholesale?

The most noble purpose for using them is to defend that which is worthy and which, it is felt, cannot be defended in any other way. Often, and tragically, this becomes the rationalization even when it isn't the reason.

Let us, however, note reasons often given and list them in ascending order.

There are those who use weapons sadistically and for obviously unworthy motives. We are not concerned here about them, for they would be condemned by just about all persons.

There are those who use weapons to protect their pride. We are reminded of James and John asking Jesus to call down destruction upon the Samaritan village, as illustrations of the danger that this motivation may afflict even honorable men.

There are those who use weapons out of fear and frustration.

There are those who use weapons or take recourse to force and violence out of lack of imagination. They have run out of ideas of better ways of resolving conflicts among individuals and groups. Confucius is reputed to have said, "He who strikes the first blow admits he has run out of ideas." We may not like all that goes on in the United Nations gatherings, but we can be thankful that they are talking and not shooting!

There are those who take weapons or use force because they feel this is the only way to protect peace and justice. If one (person or nation) is strong enough, no one will dare attack, and right and justice will be promoted. So goes this affirmation of faith.

In Plato's *Republic* there is a dialogue between Socrates and the others. They are searching for a definition of justice. As each succeeding definition is proposed, Socrates finds a flaw in it. Finally, impatiently, Thrasymachus says, "Justice is the interest of the stronger!" Is this where we are in the world today?

Why do men take the sword? For all of these reasons, some apparently worthy, some obviously unworthy.

Our second question is more important: What is accomplished by the taking of the sword—by force? There is no way of assessing what might have happened in history if different methods had been used, but I have always found provocative the statement that history is written by the survivors. This is obvious and sounds inane, at first. But think of its implications for a moment. History is written by survivors. Do not survivors automatically justify that which enabled them to survive and so equate right with what is? What of those who did not survive and so cannot plead their own cause? Since they did not survive, they must have been wrong. What is, is right! That doesn't sound so good, does it?

What is accomplished by the sword-taker that might not have been better accomplished in some other way? Was the

33

tragedy which overwhelmed this nation one hundred years ago the only solution to that problem? And after a century did it solve the problems? Regardless of past wars, we can be pretty sure that asking who won a war today is like asking who won the San Francisco earthquake! What an incredible loss of life and property, not to mention unmeasured and unmeasurable loss of potential—human and otherwise. Some years ago, I recall hearing Bernard Clausen, great Baptist preacher, refer in his sermon to an almost fatal (although unknown) encounter he had almost had with Martin Niemöller. Martin Niemöller, before becoming a church leader and chief opponent to Hitler, served in World War I as the captain of a U-boat. Bernard Clausen served in that same war on an American sub-chaser. Both men ṛ diaries. Dr. Clausen took his diary one day as he wa' ing Niemöller's biography and discovered that, on at least one occasion, Clausen's sub-chaser and Niemöller's U-boat were within range of each other. How much poorer the world would be if either or both had been successful. How much poorer the world is because so many killers were successful. Each of us has deeply personal memories. Only God can measure the cost.

In 1948 two G.I.'s wrote as follows:

Through all the ages of recorded history wars have been waged and all the multitudes who fought them believed that they were fighting for justice or right or liberty, and in the cause of these beliefs they murdered each other. Yet in the thousands of years of bloodshed, the rape of cities, the desolation of land, all prosecuted in the cause of such abstractions, nothing of worth to

34

the human spirit has come out of them. Men are no wiser than Socrates, no saintlier than Confucius, in all the twenty-five hundred years of blood-letting that stand between their day and ours. It is time to call a halt to slaughter of men and to those social forms that live by murder. It is time to address those who seek to justify war for any cause whatever and to say to them that there has been no cause of the many holy causes, no slogan of the myriad high-sounding slogans, no war of the 5000 years of war, that is worth one solitary human life.[4]

It is sometimes claimed that ends justify means. But this is absurd, because means determine ends. They cannot be separated. Jesus makes reference to the strong man who is going to be so strong and then meets someone just a little bit stronger. But more important, how do you change an idea with a club? How do you sweep darkness out of a room with a broom? How do you change a man's thoughts by killing him? Paul reminds us that we fight not against flesh and blood. The only way to destroy an enemy is to make him a friend.

The third question is more important. What does taking the sword do to the sword-wielder? It was Marcus Aurelius who wrote in his *Meditations,* "The best way to avenge yourself is not to become like the wrong-doer."

Let me share a deep concern about this nation of ours which I love dearly—too dearly to surrender my obligation to be critical of it. True love of nation is expressed in striving to improve it and bring it closer to God's will rather than accepting blindly whatever is. In 1940 a great debate raged in the United States that dealt with a fundamental issue for a democratic society. The debate was whether or not a democratic nation in peacetime could, on the basis of a great national drawing, compel certain of its citizens to carry on tasks not being filled by voluntary enlistment. Could a democracy do this in peacetime without becoming like those totalitarian nations founded upon principles diametrically opposed to ours? There was great debate and soul-searching as the world was being engulfed by flame, but while we were still technically at peace. Finally, selective service and the first peacetime military conscription in our history was enacted. This in a nation first settled by many who had fled just such conditions in their homelands. We have come through a great war. Peacetime conscription remains with us almost twenty years later. Each time the program comes up for renewal, there is virtually *no* debate. In 1963 the hearings were most desultory and only 3 out of 435 members of the House of Representatives even raised any question about it. What happens to the sword-wielder in his attitudes toward basic principles? Incidentally, if involuntary conscription is a good thing in a democracy, how about drafting teachers, nurses, social workers, and persons for other needed service occupations? Also, how about the fact that this is most discriminatory because it rules out women? However, the most distressing thing about this is that it isn't even discussed.

If anyone knows anything about war and its effects, it should be Dwight David Eisenhower. While President, he warned about the "military-industrial" complex in this country and the extent of its influence. John M. Swomley's great study on *The Military Establishment* makes for somber reading. We are all conscious of individual tragedies in the cases of men, taught to slaughter with great skill, who could not make the transition back to civilian life. Augustine wrote: "In no way can thine enemy so hurt thee by his violence as thou dost hurt thyself if thou love him not." And Arnold J. Toynbee stated, "The single art of war makes progress at the expense of all the arts of peace." [5]

The night before President Wilson asked Congress to declare war, he told Frank Cobb, editor of the New York *World*, "Once lead this people into war, and they'll forget there was ever such a thing as tolerance . . . and the spirit of ruthless brutality will enter into the very fibre of our national life."

What happens to the sword-wielder?

The fourth question is the most important. What are the alternatives in the world in which we live? The poet Whittier is credited with the statement that "peace has higher tests of manhood than battles ever knew." Often, on the individual level, the hardest thing is to refrain from striking back or to restrain the verbal violence that so easily leaps to the surface under provocation. But it is possible.

It is possible for the Christian to be free from the fear of the consequences of self-giving love, but it is not easy. It is possible to be willing to suffer rather than to inflict suffering, as was Jesus. But great faith is needed, like unto that of Gethsemane. Paul counseled us never to let evil get the better of us, but to get the better of evil by doing good. Can we destroy sin without destroying the sinner? That's the great question, isn't it? It can't be done apart from love.

In his Farewell Address George Washington held out an ideal for his nation:

It will be worthy of . . . a great nation to give to mankind the magnanimous and too novel example of a people always guided by an exalted justice and benevolence. Who can doubt that in the course of time and things the fruits of such a plan would richly repay any temporary advantages which might be lost by a steady adherence to it? Can it be that Providence has not connected the permanent felicity of a nation with its virtues? The experiment, at least, is recommended by every sentiment which ennobles human nature. . . . Antipathies against particular nations and passionate attachments for others should be excluded and . . . in place of them, just and amicable feelings toward all should be cultivated. The nation which indulges toward another an habitual hatred, or an habitual fondness, is in some degree a slave. It is a slave to its animosity or to its affection, either of which is sufficient to lead it astray from its duty and its interest.

The Rev. George Hill, while Minister of World Affairs at the Palma Ceia Methodist Church in Tampa, Florida, wrote,

When you come to grips with the basic problem that confronts the world you see that the real issue is one of self-denial. The crisis is this: Will the rich minority of which we Americans are the leaders truly share with the poor majority of the world's people? Actually it is not a question of if we will share; it is one of how we will share. Will we share willingly from our abundance, using our resources to meet the real needs of ourselves and others? Or will we continue to over-spend on self, slaves to those who make us want things we don't need, until we are forced to share or blow up the world? Will we continue to make "communism" our excuse for self-righteousness and self-centeredness, or will we see it as a challenge to meet the needs of an emerging world?

This is not a criticism of our government. Many responsible leaders recognize the situation, but far too many of our people are far behind the leaders, living in an escapist never-neverland —as rich minorities have historically done to their own destruction.*

An overwhelming proportion of the total national budget is spent each year to pay for past, present, or future wars. A two percent reduction in that would more than double what we are spending for positive programs for peace.

IV

When Jesus was asked, "Shall we strike with the sword?" he said, "Put up your sword in its place; for all who take the sword will perish by the sword." He went from there to the Crucifixion—but beyond the Crucifixion to the Resurrection!

One of the great hymns of the church sounds like a martial song. But note carefully the third and fourth lines of the second stanza of the hymn, "Lead On, O King Eternal." They read,

> For not with swords loud clashing,
>   nor roll of stirring drums;
> With deeds of love and mercy,
>   the heavenly kingdom comes.

"Shall we smite with the sword?"
Consider in closing these classic words from the lips of

one who, tradition tells us, was the only Christian to gain the presence of Saladin, the Saracen king during the Crusades, and live to tell of it. Francis of Assisi prayed:

Lord, make me an instrument of thy peace; where there is hatred, let me sow love; where there is injury, pardon; where there is doubt, faith; where there is despair, hope; where there is darkness, light; and where there is sadness, joy.

O Divine Master, grant that I may not so much seek to be consoled as to console; to be understood as to understand; to be loved as to love; for it is in giving that we receive, it is in pardoning that we are pardoned, and it is in dying that we are born to eternal life.

Thanks be to God for the privilege!

3. "What Is Truth?"

(Third Sunday in Lent)
Scripture: John 18:12-14, 19-24, 28-38

What a strange setting for what sounds almost like the start of a philosophical discussion. What a pity that he who posed the question didn't wait for an answer. Why did Pilate ask it, anyway? What sounds like a most academic question is actually a very personal one. For it reflects an eternal search.

It also reflects a universal search. Every one of us (whether or not he realizes it) is seeking for the answer to that question. Every one of us is reflecting his answer by the way he lives his life. It is, therefore, most important that we pause and consider it carefully, particularly in these changing times.

Let us think together, after we have re-created the scene, about what truth is not; what it is; and our relation to it.

I

First, then, the scene.

Recall to memory the sequence of events. Following the

41

supper in the upper room, the praying in the garden, the seizing of Jesus by the temple guard, Jesus was taken, according to the Fourth Gospel, first to Annas, the father-in-law of Caiaphas, the current high priest. Annas appears as the power behind the throne, as a former high priest himself. While Jesus was at the home of Annas, we have the first of Peter's denials out in the courtyard.

After being questioned by Annas, Jesus was taken to Caiaphas. He it was, you will remember, who had asked if it was not expedient for one man to die rather than for the entire nation to suffer. The interview before Caiaphas was unsatisfactory, however, for the leaders did not have the power to inflict the death penalty. Consequently, they took Jesus to Pilate, the Roman governor. This was humiliating, but necessary, if Jesus was to be eliminated.

Apparently he was taken to the praetorium and there turned over to the Roman guards. The Passover was approaching and they could not enter or they would become unclean. We wonder how Pilate received Jesus.

What sort of man was Pilate? Was he a frustrated cynical public official who wanted to be done with this nuisance as quickly as possible? Was he a military man, more at home on the field of battle than in the judgment hall, in a post beyond his ability? Was he simply personally ambitious, hoping to use this appointment as but one rung on the ladder upward to larger position? Was he an honest and sincere public official sincerely trying to do what was best, but caught between his feeling for justice on the one hand, and the political necessity of appeasing the leaders of the nation on the other? Did he see nothing wrong with this man and so want to set him free, but could not for fear of the upheaval and possible rioting which would look very bad on his record back in Rome?

There is no way of answering these questions, but it is interesting that he took so much time to question Jesus. Something there was that set this prisoner off from the usual run of petty revolutionaries. How did Pilate ask the question which is our text? With what intonation? If we knew that, we could answer the earlier questions. Did he, at the end of the interview, with the intonation of cynical despair say, in effect, "Oh, sure, but what is truth?" without waiting for the answer deliberately? Did he ask it seriously and musingly, but assuming there really is no answer, "What is truth?" Regardless of how Pilate asked it, it continues to plague us. "What is truth?"

II

First, let us consider what truth is not.

Truth is not just majority opinion. One of my college roommates used to maintain vehemently in those long undergraduate bull sessions that there is no ultimate and final truth but that the majority opinion of mankind establishes truth. In the social realm that has been found to be true and dependable which the majority of mankind has thought to be true. All truth, to him, was but relative. Some others have maintained this as Oliver Wendell Holmes put it, in preparing to demolish the idea, "Truth is the majority vote of that nation which can lick all the others." Perhaps, temporarily, but not over the long pull. No, truth is not just majority opinion.

43

Truth is not the authoritarian edict of some powerful group or person—whether it be the presidium of the U.S.S.R., the pope of the Roman Catholic Church, the will of Adolf Hitler, or whatever. Truth is not something defined and handed down full-blown from some authoritarian source. We are familiar with the experience of Galileo in connection with the authoritarian church of his day. The story is told that, in the latter years of his life, when he was called before the Inquisition to recant his heretical claim that the earth revolved around the sun, the elderly man did recant, probably to save himself from excruciating torture. However, he is reputed to have said under his breath, "but the earth does move!" Whether apocryphal or not, the story illustrates what happens to truth when it is assumed it can be defined by an authoritarian and rigid body.

Let us not delude ourselves, however, that this attitude ended with the Middle Ages. In 1963 there took place an event in our country which, if it were not so tragic, would be ludicrous. A basketball team which was outstanding in its part of the country was invited to take part in the National Collegiate Athletic Association tournament to determine the national champion. However, the governor and attorney general of that state obtained an injunction and issued subpoenas to prevent the boys and the coach of that team from going to Chicago to play in the tournament. The players and the coach were able to scatter so that the subpoenas could not be served, and Mississippi State did play Loyola in Chicago. Mississippi State lost, but they were certainly not disgraced, since Loyola won the tournament even though they had on their team certain players, who, according to "official truth" in Mississippi at the time, were somewhat less than fully human because of a difference of hair texture and skin pigmentation.

No, truth is not determined by authoritarian edict.

Truth is not just unsupported personal experience, either. I doubt that many of us would argue that the earth is not round. However, there are relatively few of us who have actually experienced that roundness, by traveling all around the world. So far as our unsupported personal experience is concerned, the earth is flat, or perhaps slightly domed.

While serving as chaplain in a mental hospital, I was impressed by the fact that truth is not just unsupported personal experience. There was one very gracious patient upon whom I called weekly. She was most logical and reasonable in most of her conversation. This was during World War II. Each time I visited her, sometime during our talk together she would tell me in the most straightforward fashion of the visit she had had the night before with General Douglas MacArthur—of the problems he had shared with her and the advice she had given him. She was deadly serious, even though she was on Long Island and General MacArthur was in the South Pacific.

No, truth is not just unsupported personal experience.

Truth is not just pure logic or reason by itself. It is impossible to be completely objective in our observations. We can also play tricks with ourselves, using reason and logic. The conclusion of every syllogism is presupposed in its major premise. Using logic alone, however, we can prove that something equals nothing. It is an axiom that doubles of equals are equal. Now, a glass half empty is the same as a glass half full. Therefore, since doubles of equals are equal, a glass empty is the same as a glass full! Right? Logically, perhaps, but not experientially!

Then there are the famous Pythagorean conundrums. On the basis of logic alone, an arrow shot from a bow can never reach the target. Why? Because at any moment in time, the arrow is stationary. The total amount of time is but the sum of its parts; so if the arrow is stationary at one moment it is stationary in each moment and will never move. Or, one can prove mathematically that it is impossible to leave this room. Before I can reach the door, I must cover half the distance. Then I must cover half the remainder, and then half that remainder, etc. Well, you can take half of a half of a half of a half of a half forever, and you will never reach the end.

Truth is not just unsupported logic.

Truth is not just enthusiastic sincerity. One prayed wisely, "O Lord, forgive us for being enthusiastically wrong!" There are those who substitute vehemence for veracity. There is the story of the sexton who was cleaning up after the Sunday service. He found the Pastor's sermon notes on the pulpit. He was interested to read in the margin the following: "Argument weak here; better holler!"

William Penn is credited with saying, "Truth suffers more from the heat of its defenders than from the arguments of its opposers."

No, truth is not just enthusiastic sincerity.

this, but we can experience its impact, affirm its glory and proclaim its liberating effect. This is precisely what the Christian life is all about—the proclamation that, in all things and in every way, Jesus Christ himself is truth.

IV

We now glimpse the meaning of the statement with which we began when we said that what sounds like the start of a philosophical discussion of an academic question actually poses a deeply personal one. Therefore, our relation to this question can no longer be in terms of the intellectual give and take, but in terms of fundamental, personal commitment.

If I truly believe that Jesus Christ is truth, then I am going to stake my whole life on it. I will be strengthened and emboldened for the adventure that the quest is, realizing with James Russell Lowell that

> New occasions teach new duties;
>   Time makes ancient good uncouth;
> They must upward still, and onward,
>   who would keep abreast of Truth;
> Lo, before us gleam her camp-fires!
>   we ourselves must Pilgrims be,
> Launch our Mayflower, and steer boldly
>   through the desperate winter sea,
> Nor attempt the Future's portal
>   with the Past's blood-rusted key.[*]

It's a quest; it's an adventure; it's a commitment. Also, it frees, or sets free, as Jesus said. Some of this freedom is reflected in the words of the woman who said to her therapist, "Doctor, do you realize the happiest day of my life was the day when—after a number of talks with you— I stopped trying to look twenty years younger than I am!" This freedom from the false opens the way to the commitment reflected in these words of Harold Cooke Phillips: "In moral reality, then, lies the keystone of the arch of life. No civilization has ever fallen because it lacked knowledge, but invariably because it lacked character. The great crises of life are induced not so much because men lack intelligence as because they lack integrity."

Our faith, then involves four affirmations:

First: God is the only source of truth. In fact, God, is, by definition, the source of being and meaning.

Second: Any honest search for truth will only bring us closer to God. Therefore, no sincere honest question is inappropriate. It was this conviction, given me by an admired Christian leader, which guided me safely over my own adolescent struggles with atheism.

Third: Truth will ultimately triumph if we will commit ourselves to the search.

Fourth: The important question is what shall be the extent of my commitment to the search?

V

Three thoughts in closing:

In a manual prepared for church school teachers there appeared a statement which has stuck in my mind. It went something like this: "It is not enough to know the truth. One must be the truth."

Edwin Markham wrote

> Here is the truth in a little creed,
>   Enough for all the roads we go:
> In love is all the law we need,
>   In Christ is all the God we know.[4]

Finally, let us make our own the ancient prayer:

> From the cowardice that shrinks from new truth,
> From the laziness that is content with half-truths,
> From the arrogance that thinks it knows all truth,
>   O God of Truth, deliver us.

4. "What Shall I Do with Jesus Who Is Called Christ?"

THE INESCAPABLE QUESTION

(Fourth Sunday in Lent)
Scripture: Matt. 27:11-31

Whether he was a wily politician trying to get out of a difficult predicament or a conscientious public leader striving to bring a crowd or mob to its senses, Pilate asked a question which cannot be avoided. He may have tried to evade his responsibility but did not succeed. Neither can we.

Let us think together about this question asked by Pilate in the midst of the suffering of Jesus at his trial in the praetorium. He asked the crowd, "What shall I do with Jesus who is called Christ?" This is the inescapable question still ringing down the centuries. Everyone, whether consciously or unconsciously, answers it. Consider, then, the scene, some answers that have been given, and a rephrasing of the question.

I

First, the scene: You remember the events that have led up to this—the upper room, the garden, the betrayal, the seizing, the private conference between Jesus and Pilate. Pilate takes Jesus out before the crowd. What a strange figure he presents as he stands up there on his balcony trying to temporize, trying to evade the responsibility for the decision that seems to be forced upon him. See this man representing the might of the Roman empire, asking the advice of the mob! How strange he looks. Pilate, however, is trying to avoid his responsibility; so his voice does not reflect the might and power of Rome and certain basic justice, but becomes merely an echo for the passions of the mob. Three times he tries to extricate himself from this difficult situation, caught as he is between his own feeling that Jesus is innocent and the threat of a political riot.

First, he offers the crowd a choice by bringing out another famous prisoner, whom we know as Barabbas. Reminding the crowd of the custom to set a man free on the festival day, he asks which of the two they will have. It is interesting to note that in some of the oldest manuscripts the given name of Barabbas is recorded as being the same as that of the man from Nazareth. The word "barabbas" simply means "son of a father" and was presumably the alias of this bandit and insurrectionist. Assuming the same given name for each prisoner heightens the drama, does it not? For now we see Pilate asking the crowd, "Which will you have, Jesus, the 'son of a father' or Jesus, the Son of man?" If we remember, further, that the word "Jesus" itself is an adaptation of the name "Joshua," meaning "Yahweh saves," then the question becomes even more profound. Which way will you follow for salvation? Which way does Yahweh save? Through violence, through pillage, through killing as represented by this "son of a father" or through forgiveness, through sacrifice, through love as represented by this "Son of man"? Yes, a provocative thought. Which will you have? The mob shouts for Barabbas, and Pilate's first attempt to evade responsibility fails.

He tries again. "Then what shall I do with Jesus who is called Christ?" There comes rolling back that spine-chilling shout, "Crucify!" The events of the Passion have been set to music by many. In each a climax in the musical rendition causes chills to run up and down the spine as the choir, echoing the mob, shouts, "Crucify!" "Why? What harm has he done?" But again, "Crucify!" Pilate's second attempt at evasion comes to naught.

He makes a third attempt. In so doing he has given us a common figure of speech. He calls for a basin of water and in front of the crowd washes his hands. "I am innocent of the blood of this just man. Ever since, "to wash one's hands" of something has meant to repudiate responsibility for it. He says further, "I am innocent of the blood of this just man." Then comes the horrible shout, "Let his blood be on us and our children!"

Pilate's attempts to evade responsibility have come to nothing. The decision has been forced upon him. He has Jesus scourged and crucified. Sometimes we overlook the scourging, forgetting that this was a process by which a cat-o-nine-tails into the thongs of which had been braided bits of jagged metal was laid upon the bare back of the victim so that he was left a mass of quivering flesh. There was the scourging, the mocking, and then he was taken away to be crucified.

Even as Pilate could not evade his responsibility, so we cannot evade the question which comes down the centuries. "What shall I do with Jesus who is called Christ?" "What shall we in the Christian church, what shall we as a society, do with Jesus who is called Christ?"

II

Consider some answers that have been given to this question down through the centuries.

There are those who have admired the man Jesus; who have looked up to this fine person; who have gone so far as to worship him, setting him up on pedestals. They have said in effect, "He was marvelous, a brave man, much more than a man, the Son of God. But let's not be impractical and expect to live the way he suggested. We must postpone the application of the life that he came to bring until everybody else is ready to live that way, too. He was a good man, and certainly the Golden Rule is a marvelous ideal, and the Sermon on the Mount is interesting, but let's be practical. Certainly you don't expect an intelligent person in this world to turn the other cheek; to love and forgive our enemies; to love everybody. When the perfect society comes, yes; but certainly not now!" Yes, men have answered in this way in terms of admiration and worship, but postponing the Christian life, overlooking the fact that when the per-

55

fect society comes forgiveness for enemies won't be necessary since there won't be any (!) and overlooking the fact that the best way to bring in the kingdom of God is to act as though it were already here. For it actually is; we only need to respond to it. But some have admired, worshiped, and patronized.

Some have handled the question by trying to ignore it and by trying to ignore the fact of Jesus Christ. But, as Halford Luccock has written:

We must not imagine that ignoring him is the same thing as escaping him. We can no more escape Jesus by ignoring him than we can escape dying by ignoring death. We can, however, blot him out of our lives and go on as though he had never lived, and as though he had never died. In doing so we will blot out our highest and richest potentialities. The gospel is the good news that we can, if we will, accept him and follow him.[1]

One of the greatest problems that any pastor or church group faces is how to get across to the persons who just aren't interested the fact of the revelation of the nature of God in Jesus Christ. Of all the frustrations, this is the greatest: the plight of the person who is self-satisfied and will just not recognize his own need. Where are the other two thirds of the perfectly healthy members of Protestant churches across this nation any Sunday morning who are not in their pews?

G. A. Studdert-Kennedy of Birmingham, England, famous World War I chaplain, wrote a poem for his own parish in England and expressed something of this thought:

WHAT SHALL I DO WITH JESUS WHO IS CALLED CHRIST?

When Jesus came to Golgotha they hanged him to a tree,
They drave great nails through hands and feet, and made a
Calvary;
They crowned him with a crown of thorns, red were his wounds
and deep,
For those were crude and cruel days, and human flesh was
cheap.

When Jesus came to Birmingham [or New Haven?], they simply
passed him by,
They never hurt a hair of him, they only let him die;
For men had grown more tender, and they would not give him
pain,
They only just passed down the street, and left him in the rain.

Still Jesus cried, "Forgive them for they know not what they
do,"
And still it rained the winter rain that drenched him through
and through;
The crowds went home and left the streets without a soul to see,
And Jesus crouched against a wall and cried for Calvary.[2]

Some ignore him.

Then there are those who have deliberately rejected him
—who have turned their backs on him and said he is wrong.
They have crucified him afresh in this rejection. Periodical-
ly I reread that fantasy in *The Brothers Karamazov* by
Dostoevsky called the "Grand Inquisitor." You remember
that Ivan is sketching for his brother the outline of an epic
poem that he plans to write some day. It takes the shape of
an interview between the Grand Inquisitor in Seville,
Spain, and Jesus who has returned to the earth in the fif-
teenth century. In the course of the interview Jesus never

speaks. This is actually a long soliloquy by the Grand Inquisitor. In the course of it he points out to Jesus what a fool he was and how the church now has (catch this phrase) "corrected thy work." Jesus was a fool because he gave men freedom to choose. Anyone should know, the Grand Inquisitor points out, that man is not intelligent enough to use his freedom. Jesus in his temptation refused to give the people bread and refused to do miracles to impress them, but the church knows better. It has done things for man's good, because he is not able to handle freedom. The Grand Inquisitor goes on and tells how he "turned back and joined the ranks of those who have corrected thy mistakes." At the very end of the interview, having stirred himself to a climax, he says, "Tomorrow, I shall burn thee. I have spoken." We have here the picture of Jesus coming back after fifteen centuries and being slain once more as an obstacle to mankind. At the very end of this fantasy, Jesus still does not speak, but steps forward and kisses the Inquisitor before he is led away. Yes, some have rejected him by correcting his mistakes.

"What shall I do with Jesus, who is called Christ?" Admire, worship, patronize, ignore, reject, and crucify afresh?

III

Happily, this is not the whole story. Through the ages there have been many whose answer has been to follow him, after surrendering to him; what an endless line of splendor and glory this is! These have transformed the world.

Simon, the fisherman, a "sandpile" of a man, given to sudden enthusiasm with no stability whatever, was transformed into the "rock-man." Saul, the Pharisee, persecuting the Christians, responded and became Paul, the apostle. A young man in North Africa, a libertine and searcher after pleasure, was transformed by his Christian faith, and Augustine could write, "Thou hast made us for thyself so that our souls are restless until they find rest in thee" and could pen, as the Roman empire was crashing to pieces around him, a vision of "the city of God" set over against the crumbling world around. A young man from a wealthy family in Italy responded and prayed, "Lord, make me an instrument of thy peace" and is known and revered as Francis of Assisi.

There was a young lawyer in northwestern Europe who was so frightened over the ultimate destiny of his own soul that he made a vow during a thunderstorm that he would become a monk if his life were spared. Martin Luther's study and devotion led him to challenge the might of the church and the Holy Roman Empire with the declaration, "Here I stand. God helping me, I can do no other." A thirty-five-year-old English college graduate, university tutor, Anglican priest, with many of the honors of the world and much of the status and prestige that comes with outstanding scholarly accomplishment, but knowing within his own heart he was a failure, finds his "heart strangely warmed" and John Wesley embarks on a career which changed the lives of thousands with whom he came into contact and millions more who came after.

There was a young Baptist cobbler, in the later years of the eighteenth century, who, while sitting at a conference, raised the question whether or not the commission of Jesus to go into all the world applied to those present. He heard the chairman say, "Sit down, you miserable enthusiast. When God is ready to convert the heathen, he will do it without your help." But, though William Carey sat down that day, he did not remain seated. Self-educated, he traveled up and down the length and breadth of England preaching a great sermon over and over again. Many times I have heard the two points of this sermon quoted, but usually in the reverse order from the way he preached them. William Carey's points were: "Expect great things from God; attempt great things for God." He went to India and wrought mightily for his Lord.

There was the son of a wealthy family in Japan who became a Christian and was disowned. I remember hearing him speak to a large meeting when I was a young boy, while he was visiting in this country. He joked about his poor English and said, "You see my English is not good because my teeth were made by a Japanese dentist!" He had lost his own teeth because of disease and the suffering he had undergone in the slums of Kobe, which also left him with sadly impaired sight. But, Toyohiko Kagawa could write: "God is love! I will proclaim this until I fall. God is love! I do not mean that the unseen God is love. Where love is, there is God!"

There is a Doctor of Philosophy, a Doctor of Theology, a Doctor of Music, the world's foremost authority on organ building and the works of Bach, an outstanding authority on the works of Goethe, who, in his middle thirties gave up all this, became a Doctor of Medicine and went to Africa to repay God something of the goodness he had received.

There are those who would say that Albert Schweitzer was a fool, throwing his life away. He would answer differently.

There was the young pastor who chose not to abandon his teaching in time of danger during the Third Reich and whose writings from prison speak to many in our present generation, so that Dietrich Bonhoeffer's influence is very much alive in these days.

We can multiply by the millions the names of those who, when asked, "What shall I do with Jesus who is called Christ?" have followed after him, knowing that:

> If our love were but more simple
> We should take him at his word;
> And our lives would be all sunshine
> In the sweetness of our Lord.[3]

but knowing also, that we have posed the question incorrectly. These have not followed in their own strength alone, but because they have submitted to Christ.

IV

Let us, therefore, rephrase our question. The question really is, "What shall I allow Jesus, who is called Christ, to do with me?" "What shall I allow him to do through me?" The answer to the old traditional question, "What must I do to be saved?" is not to earn it in some way, but to receive it and so be saved from anxiety, from self-concern, from suffering, from the limitedness of our lives. How? The traditional answers to the question point the direction to the answer of the other question, "What shall I allow Jesus, who is called Christ, to do with me?"

First, we must recognize our need. This is one aspect, at least, of repentance. Second, believe, trust, accept. I still remember that community Thanksgiving service at which I heard Russell Henry Stafford make what seemed to me an incredible statement. He said, "God is like Jesus. Therefore, nothing is too good to be true and nothing bad can be final." I recall saying to myself, "Wait a minute; that's a little too much." Yet this is precisely the claim that we make as Christians. Audacious, but true. God *is* like Jesus; therefore, nothing is too good to be true, and nothing bad can be final.

G. A. Studdert-Kennedy again:

> . . . I bet my life on beauty, truth,
> And love! not abstract, but incarnate truth;
> Not beauty's passing shadow, but its self,
> Its very self made flesh—love realized.
> I bet my life on Christ, Christ crucified,
> Aye risen, and alive forevermore.[4]

Recognize need; believe and trust and then there will follow certain results, certain fruit. First will come confidence as we realize that the results of life are with God. Does not so much of despair in human life come from impatience because we cannot know the final results of all that we do? The hymn reminds us, "one step enough for me," but do we believe it? Jesus said much the same thing in the Sermon on the Mount. I remember hearing Sherwood Eddy in a men's corporate communion service describe our human condition as like that of a man in pitch blackness but with a small flashlight strapped to his foot. The light will shine about two feet forward. If the man stands still and waits for the surrounding darkness to go away, he may stand there forever. But if he steps forward the light will advance with him and illuminate the next step. The one step will then be seen to be doubly worthwhile.

A traveler stopped a little boy and said, "Have you ever been to Boston? How do I get there?" The boy replied, "I've never been to Boston, but there's the road to it." Have you ever been in the kingdom of God or in the perfect society? No, but here's the road to it.

> "How far that little candle throws his beams!
> So shines a good deed in a naughty world." [5]

Have we the confidence that doing the little right is worthwhile even when the results seem to be out of sight? "What shall I allow Jesus who is called Christ to do with me?" Use me as a planter of seeds that may come to fruition later? Use me as leaven that must lose itself in the loaf to do any good?

A statement that came to my attention years ago has had considerable influence on my thinking. It is this: We are not punished so much *for* our sins as *by* them. And I proclaim to you that the reverse is also true: We are not rewarded so much *for* our virtues—*for* our good deeds—as *by* them, for they are a result of the answer to the rephrased question.

Another result that will follow is the need (and the ability) to share the glorious good news.

Whenever there is silence around me
By day or by night—
I am startled by a cry.
It came down from the cross—
The first time I heard it.
I went out and searched—
And found a Man in the throes of crucifixion,
And I said, "I will take You down,"
And I tried to take the nails out of His feet.
But He said, "Let them be
For I cannot be taken down
Until every man, every woman, and every child
Come together to take Me down."
And I said, "But I cannot hear You cry.
What can I do?"
And He said, "Go about the world—
Tell everyone that you meet—
There is a Man on the cross
Waiting for them to take Him down." *

"What will I allow Jesus who is called Christ to do with me?" We will share by words, through the fellowship of the church, through the personalities that we are.

V

Consider this expanded paraphrase of some words of Jesus: If anyone wants to go with me, let him disregard himself and his limited desires and purposes and let him take up his redemptive service in response to me, taking gladly whatever burdens have come to him and follow the example I have given. For whoever wants only to preserve his own life as an end in itself and serve only his own desires and limited purposes will find that his life becomes worthless even to himself. But whoever gives his life gladly to me will find that it has become a glorious experience, full of purpose, peace, and joy. For what shall it profit a person if he gain the whole world of material things but throws away, in the process, all eternal meaning and purpose?

"What shall I do with Jesus who is called Christ?"

"What will I allow Jesus who is called Christ to do with and through me?"

5. "My God, Why?"

THE QUESTION FROM SUFFERING

(Fifth Sunday in Lent or Passion Sunday)
Scripture: Mark 15:21-39

"My God, why?" Echoing down the ages and reverberating in the heart of every person who has ever suffered deeply is the agonizing question, "Why?" Why has this happened? Why did this happen to me?

Along with the agony of the question is the bewilderment at how God can be conceived of as both all-loving and all-powerful. If God is all-loving, he cannot be all-powerful, since there is suffering. If God is all-powerful, he cannot be all-loving since he allows suffering. How to resolve the dilemma, mirrored on the cross and experienced so deeply by so many?

The fifth Sunday in Lent is often known as Passion Sunday. It has been designated as the Sunday on which we think together about the meaning and the purpose of the suffering of Jesus, and, by extension, something of the meaning and purpose of our own.

Lenten observances have evolved through the centuries,

from a forty-hour observance at first; then to include all of Holy Week; then a tithe (or tenth) of the year; and finally our present observance of forty days before Easter, exclusive of Sundays. The nature of the observance has evolved as well. If one uses the Lenten period for consideration of the events of the last week in chronological sequence, then Palm Sunday comes as an interruption. You cannot put Palm Sunday at the beginning of Lent, nor does it seem appropriate to think too much about the suffering of Jesus on this day of triumphant entry. Consequently, the Sunday before Palm Sunday has been designated as Passion Sunday.

We shall think together about the cry of Jesus from the cross as recorded in Matthew and Mark. We shall then consider three attitudes toward suffering and conclude with four affirmations.

I

It is interesting to note that of the seven statements attributed to Jesus on the cross, only Matthew and Mark record the question "Why?" Luke records three others, not found elsewhere, and John also has three not found elsewhere. Traditional Good Friday services have long grouped these seven with three statements for others—the word of forgiveness and word to the penitent thief (Luke) and the word to John and Jesus' mother (John)—followed by the cry that sounds at first like a cry of despair, but which may be more. The other three statements are the word of thirst and the statement that it is finished (John), with the word

67

of commendation (Luke), quoting from Psalm 31, as the conclusion.

These statements are preceded by the taunts of the crowd and the scribes. They seem to have missed the point, when they taunt him for not leaving the cross, that he need not have assumed it. He could very easily have escaped at any of several points along the journey. Indeed, this seems the center of the struggle in the garden those few hours earlier. But what means the cry, sometimes called the cry of dereliction? "My God, why hast thou forsaken me?"

Was this a cry wrenched from his lips by the agony of physical suffering? After all, his flesh bled and his nerves recorded pain, even as yours and mine. A scene from a French motion picture of the crucifixion seen many years ago has never left me. The movie-maker was an artist, and, instead of showing the raw brutalty of the flogging in the dungeon prior to the Crucifixion, he made his point indirectly. During the scourging the camera focused on a small barred window set high up in the wall of the chamber where Jesus was being tortured. At the bars of the window appeared the frenzied, hatred-filled faces of those who had shouted for his crucifixion. As the scourging begins, they enjoy the violence and brutality. But as the whipping continues, gradually the expressions change. They begin to look nauseated, and the faces drop away from the window in sickness. I've never forgotten that scene as a commentary on the physical agony.

The spiritual agony must have been even worse. As he hung on the cross he was taunted by those who passed by. He was forsaken by those closest to him. He saw his executioners tossing dice for his garments, and it may be that these things called to his memory something he had learned as a child and perhaps repeated many times. We all know how in times of stress often words of a hymn or words of a poem, or some statement made years before and buried in memory, comes to the surface as an expression of our feeling. The words of the cry from the cross are the first words of Psalm 22. This psalm also reflects the psalmist's feeling of being taunted and forsaken and includes the statement, "they divide my garments among them, and for my raiment they cast lots" (vs. 18).

Did this combination of factors call this ancient song to the consciousness of Jesus? He had now hung on the cross for six hours, we are told. Exhaustion was beginning to take its toll. These words came to his lips. Are they words of loneliness or despair? Or are they something else?

If you will examine the psalm, you will discover that it has two parts. There is, first, a lament, in which the writer of the psalm and presumably those who used it in ritual worship later are counting over the things that have happened to them that have cast them down. They recount the suffering. They are lamenting their misfortune before God and asking his help. Note they are not rejecting God. They are not saying that because these things have happened, they assume there is no God. No, they are calling God to witness and calling to him for help, reminding God that their fathers trusted in him and beseeching him to aid them as well.

In the accounts we have Jesus repeated only the first words of this psalm. Is it not possible that the whole thrust of the psalm may well have been in his mind, even as we often recapture a whole idea through speaking but an initial phrase? We shall consider the implications of this later. Before leaving the lament, think about attitudes which are taken toward suffering. "My God, in the face of my suffering, why?"

II

The first and easiest explanation of suffering is that it comes as a result of punishment for wrongdoing—punishment for sin. Of course, this does happen. If I sin against good sense and put my hand in a fire, it will be burned. I'm punished for my foolishness or for my sin against good sense. If I sin against intelligent rules of health, I will be punished by sickness and disease. Certain suffering follows sin against intelligence, sin against moral law, and who is there to argue that the difficulties we are having in our nation today—the social and ethnic upheaval—are not to some extent the result of the evil which preceded it—the sin against personality?

Yes, some suffering is punishment, but the reverse is not necessarily true. It is not true to say that since evil causes suffering, therefore, all suffering comes from prior evildoing. It was this erroneous assumption which led Job's "comforters" to argue so with him. Job insisted that he had done nothing to deserve his suffering, but his friends, over and over and in many different ways, kept insisting, "Ah, Job, you must have sinned, else this suffering would not have come to you." This is not necessarily true.

Jesus referred to the problem of undeserved suffering

70

in Luke 13 where he made reference to a tower that fell accidentally and killed many people. He asked, in effect, "Were all who died equally guilty?" In another case, that of the man born blind (John 9), he raises the question, "What sin did he commit which would cause him to be blind from birth?" When we look at that Japanese city which was wiped out with the first atom bomb, must we assume that all those who lost their lives and those who suffered such horrible mutilation were equally guilty? Where was the guilt, anyway? Sin causes suffering, but not all suffering comes from sin.

A second attitude toward the fact of pain and suffering is that it may be educational. It may serve as warning. Surely, the pain I feel when I burn my hand in the fire teaches me not to repeat the action! Incidentally, though we shrink from pain, think for a moment how horrible it would be if we did not have the protection of pain reaction. Yes, pain and suffering may serve as warnings.

Pain may also be disciplinary. After all, a muscle is only developed by overcoming resistance. Even as metal receives its fine temper only by being subjected to intense heat, so the human spirit requires tempering in the fires of adversity. The capacity to suffer is the measure of a sentient being. Without being able to suffer, one cannot sense the true meaning of life. Jesus said, "Blessed are those who mourn." That is, only the person who can enter into the suffering of others has the sensitivity to be able to receive comfort and strength himself. "Blessed are those who mourn, for they shall be comforted." (Matt. 5:4.)

We may learn and grow from suffering. Life is not so

71

much what happens *to* us as what happens *in* us. If you dabble in photography you know that all light makes no picture. There is an Arab proverb that all sun makes a desert. There often comes to mind the story of Jacob wrestling with the angel (Gen. 32). Without becoming involved in the legendary framework of the story, I am always struck by one point—Jacob's insistence that "I will not let you go until you bless me." I will not relinquish this experience, whatever it may be, until I have extracted blessing from it. Suffering may be punishment; suffering may be educational; but suffering may also be redemptive.

The third attitude toward suffering is to look for the positive redemptive note in it. It is possible, through the grace of God, for such experiences to be transmuted into creative, redemptive power. In the biological realm the traditional illustration is the pearl in the oyster. More than a superficial story, this is an enduring parable. The Isaiah of the Exile, in his figure of the suffering servant, has presented in poetic form the figure of one who took upon himself the undeserved suffering and was able to transmute it into redemptive power. The perfect example is the Christ upon the cross.

There are others who have been able to use their own suffering and the new insight gained thereby to become redemptive agents for others: the parents of cerebral palsy victims who continue their concern for cerebral palsy after the death of their own child; the families who banded together after World War II—families of veterans whose faces were mutilated in combat and who had lived through the agony of readjustment to this most difficult of mutilations—but who banded together to help others through the same suffering. There are the families of mental hospital patients who assist others in rehabilitation. Examples could be multiplied of persons who have used apparently undeserved suffering to assist others.

This brings us to the interesting fact that in the New Testament we seldom, if ever, find the question raised as to why there should be suffering. The characteristic New Testament attitude is "How can this be used?" Jesus never took the time to explain philosophically why there should be suffering. Even that Old Testament book which struggles with the question, finally comes out with a leap of faith. Perhaps there is no intellectually complete answer to the question of suffering. For the Christian the question becomes of this, as of all experiences, "How can I use it to further God's purpose." The figure on the cross is the supreme example of innocent suffering being transmuted into redemptive power.

The following poem is applicable:

> The cry of earth's anguish went up unto God,—
> "Lord, take away pain,—
> The shadow that darkens the world Thou hast made
> That close-coiling chain
> That strangles the heart, the burden that weighs
> On the wings that would soar,—
> Lord, take away pain from the world Thou hast made
> That it love Thee the more."
>
> Then answered the Lord to the world He had made,
> "Shall I take away pain?

And with it the power of the soul to endure
    Made strong by the strain?
Shall I take away pity that knits heart to heart
    And sacrifice high?
Will ye lose all your heroes who lift from the flame
    White brows to the sky?
Shall I take away love that redeems with a price
    And smiles through the loss,—
Can ye spare the lives that would climb unto mine
    The Christ on His Cross?" [1]

III

Let us move to affirmation. This, of necessity, must be the affirmations of others. They are shared in the knowledge that suffering always poses two alternatives. In the face of it one may complain and give up. Or one can accept the lack of knowledge and understanding and go on serene in the confidence that God will sustain and use, even this, to his glory. That is an affirmation of faith.

In his monumental volume on Job in *The Anchor Bible* series, Marvin Pope writes as follows at the conclusion of his introduction:

Any hope a man may put in anything other than [the] First and Last One is vain. There is nothing else that abides. This is God. . . . From Him we come and to Him we return. Confidence in this One is the only value not subject to time.

But how can a man put his faith in such an One . . . ? Faith in Him is not achieved without moral struggle and spiritual agony. The foundation of such a faith has to be laid in utter despair of reliance on any or all lesser causes and in resignation which has faced and accepted the worst and the best life can

74

offer. . . . Job's journey from despair to faith is the way each mortal must go. . . . Only by faith can . . . seeming defeat be turned to victory and the anguished cry, "My God, why have you forsaken me?" give way to resignation and trust, "Father, into your hands I commend my spirit." The scribal sage who altered Job's defiant protest, "He may slay me, I'll not quaver" to read, "Though he slay me, yet will I trust in him" did so advisedly in the knowledge that this was the attitude to which Job must be driven at last.[2]

Is not this the attitude to which all of us must be driven at last?

Following the lament of the first part of Psalm 22, there comes a hymn of thanksgiving for the assurance that God does sustain. Toward the end of the psalm these words:

> All the ends of the earth shall remember
> and turn to the Lord;
> and all the families of the nations
> shall worship before him.
> For dominion belongs to the Lord,
> and he rules over the nations. (vss. 27-28)

Also, following this psalm from which Jesus quoted comes, "The Lord is my shepherd . . ." Can we not assume that the cry from the Cross is more than an utterance of despair? Is not there implied the ringing affirmation of the latter part of Psalm 22 as well?

Commenting on the New Testament, Harry Emerson Fosdick wrote:

The New Testament itself is full of trouble. It begins with a massacre of innocent children; it is centered in the crucifixion;

it ends with a vision in which the souls of the martyred saints under the altar cry, "How long, O Master?" The Book was written by men whose familiar experiences were excommunications, persecutions, martyrdoms. Their faith was not like a candle flame, easily blown out by a high wind, but like a great fire fanned into a more powerful conflagration. In consequence, while the New Testament is supremely a book of hardship and tragedy, it is far and away the most exultant and jubilant book in the literature of religion.[3]

Hear the apostle Paul:

"More than that, we rejoice in our sufferings, knowing that suffering produces endurance, and endurance produces character, and character produces hope, and hope does not disappoint us, because God's love has been poured into our hearts" (Rom. 5:3-5).

"I consider that the sufferings of this present time are not worth comparing with the glory that is to be revealed to us." (Rom. 8:18.)

"We know that in everything God works for good with those who love him" (Rom. 8:28).

"Can anything separate us from the love of Christ? Can trouble, pain or persecution? . . . I have become absolutely convinced that neither death nor life . . . nor anything else in God's whole world has any power to separate us from the love of God in Jesus Christ our Lord!" (Rom. 8:35, 38-39 Phillips.)

IV

The question rings down the centuries. "My God, why?" It reverberates in our hearts, but it can change from despair to hope. There will always be suffering, and there is no final intellectually satisfying explanation. Some suffering comes as punishment; some as education and discipline; some is redemptive. The question for the Christian is, "How can I prevent or alleviate suffering in others, and how can I use my own?"

Then we, too, may move from the despairing "My God, why?" to the confident, "Father, into thy hands I commend my spirit," knowing that this statement is not an epitaph, but a description of the Christian life.

6. "Who Is This?"

THE QUESTION FROM THE WORLD

(Palm Sunday)
Scripture: Matt. 21:1-11

"Hosanna!" How many times have we sung it or heard it sung? But what does it mean? What significance does it have for us? Does it mean simply, "Hurrah" or "Bravo" or "Bully"? Does it have just the connotation of superficial, unthinking praise and response to enthusiasm? Or does it have a deeper meaning?

Reconstruct the scene in your mind. See thousands of people coming from all over the ancient world—from all the lands of the Dispersion—up to the city to celebrate what was, at once their greatest religious festival and their greatest patriotic observance—the Passover. How many hundreds? How many thousands? There is no way of knowing. But, sense something of the joy and sense of uplift as they came over the top of the hill and saw for the first time, the city of Jerusalem spread before them.

Associated with the Passover are the Hallel psalms, numbered 113 through 118 in our Bibles. It may well be that the pilgrims sang these as they walked, or recited them to one another. At the very least, the phrases from them echoed in their minds. At any rate, the words we so easily associate with Palm Sunday, included in this chapter's Scripture, come from Psalm 118. It begins:

> "O give thanks to the Lord, for he is good;
> his steadfast love endures for ever!"

Beginning at vs. 25 are the words: "Save now, I beseech thee, O Lord: O Lord, I beseech thee, send now prosperity. Blessed be he that cometh in the name of the Lord" (KJV).

The word in this passage which, in the King James Version, is translated "save now" and, in the Revised Standard Version, is translated "save us" is the word, "Hosanna." "Hosanna" is not just a superficial cry of a crowd such as the cheering section at a football game, saying "Hurrah." It means, "save us" or "save now" or "may the Lord save." This may have meant, "May the Lord save him," or "May the Lord save through him."

How many persons were involved in this hailing of Jesus as he entered in symbolic fashion, we cannot know, but apparently the news of his coming spread around the city. Many wondered what it was all about. This question from the curious is the basis for our thought together. We read, "All the city was stirred, saying, 'Who is this?'" (Matt. 21:10.)

We shall examine the answers given to this question from the world on that occasion, answers that have been given in retrospect, and the answer for our day and its implications.

79

I

There were three answers given that day.

The immediate answer was to identify him as "the prophet Jesus from Nazareth of Galilee." A prophet is not just a fortune-teller who can read the future. A prophet is one who speaks for God. The Old Testament prophets' characteristic opening phrase was, "Thus saith the Lord." Some of the crowd, then, recognized him as a spokesman for God, whether or not they fully comprehended his message.

Earlier the crowd had sung from Psalm 118 and identified him as "Son of David" or king. He was descended from David after the flesh and also after the spirit. We often miss the full meaning of "king," if we think only in terms of inherited power, or some prerogatives received by birth. The word in our language comes from a root meaning one who can or is able. Without pinning too much on this etymology, the thought is provocative that, as king, he was one who was able. Did the crowd sense this? Did each put his own private interpretation on what he was able for?

The third answer of the day itself is reflected in the symbolism of the method of entry. Borrowing from the vision of the prophet Zechariah, Jesus entered the city, not riding on a stallion or charger or royal camel, but on a donkey. He did not choose a symbol of power and might, but a beast of burden, humble servant of mankind. He comes not as agent of vengeance, but humble as agent of peace and reconciliation.

Prophet, son of David and king, bringer of peace—these were the verbal answers and symbolic answers given in his day to the question from the world.

II

In retrospect other answers were given. We read in one of the Gospel accounts, "His disciples did not understand this at first; but when Jesus was glorified, then they remembered that this had been written of him and had been done to him." (John 12:16.)

As we look back through the centuries, we are puzzled to understand why the Palm Sunday procession took place at all. Why did Jesus enter the city in this way? Was it planned in advance, and what did it signify? The conversation that passed between Jesus and the disciples and the instructions that he gave them before going to get the colt indicate that some advance preparation had been made, or, at least, that Jesus knew what was going to happen. But why? This entry seems out of character, somehow. Also, why the change in five short days? For some of those who shouted "Hosanna" may well have shouted "crucify" later.

Did he allow the procession as a way of proclaiming his messiahship? As we study the Scriptures we discover that in some instances Jesus appeared to reveal himself as the Messiah to his disciples, but told them not to tell anyone. Did he participate in this demonstration to reveal to a wider group his true purpose? Others had proclaimed their leadership and been hailed in this way and been thought by some to be the Messiah. Zerubbabel and Judas Maccabaeus are but two examples.

Or, was the demonstration a spontaneous reaction by his followers? Perhaps they felt it necessary to express something of the joy within them caused by the fervor of the

81

Passover season and their sense of the uniqueness of their master.

Was it perhaps an acted parable through which Jesus sought to show the futility of this kind of superficial praise? Lloyd C. Douglas in his book *The Robe* has a description of this entry which shows Jesus oddly detached from the crowd with a look almost of sorrow on his face. Then there is the fact that he wept over the city before entering it. Was it a symbolic act to show the people that this is not the way?

Was it an attempt to express something of joy—even relaxation and the plaudits of the crowd—before the suffering that Jesus saw before him? These four suggestions may point the direction for provocative thought.

There still remains the tragic question, why the change in five days? On that tragic Friday he carried out the act through which God does save us; we recall that the meaning of Hosanna is "save now" or "save us." He is the message. This is the way by which salvation comes—not riding the donkey and accepting the praise of men's lips, but taking up the cross and going beyond it. Men have rejected this because they have not wanted to be changed. It is easier to sing praises with one's lips than to accept new disciplines in one's life. In the face of new truth and new requirements some, usually a small minority, try to change and adopt the new truth. Some try to ignore it. Some turn upon the bringer of the new truth and try to destroy him.

He came to bring peace. How, in our day, is this to come about? Does peace come only through the action of governments? Or does it come in some other way? In 1915 there was established an international fellowship dedicated to the proposition that a Christian has a responsibility to work for the reconciliation of those who are at odds one with the other. The members took seriously the statement that "God was in Christ reconciling the world to himself, . . . and entrusting to us the message of reconciliation. So we are ambassadors for Christ" (II Cor. 5:19-20). This organization is known as the Fellowship of Reconciliation. Although not specifically nor institutionally attached to a church, it is composed of committed Christians working for reconciliation among classes, among races and among nations. Although small, this group has had a great leavening influence in the last half century. On January 10, 1963, it became the victim of an edict handed down by the Internal Revenue Service which said that no longer could this organization enjoy tax exempt status as a religious organization, which meant that contributions to it could no longer be deducted from income tax. Many months later this ruling was changed. The incident is introduced here that we may consider the reasons given for removing the exemption.

The Internal Revenue Service offered two fantastic reasons . . . : 1) The pursuit of peace, disarmament and the reconciliation of nations is not religious but political activity. 2) The fellowship's objective—world peace—can be secured only by passage of legislation, hence the fellowship falls into a recently created category of "action organizations." [1]

Religion has nothing to do with peace and reconciliation and the only way peace can be achieved is to pass laws about it!

83

In an article entitled "Computing Jesus' Back Taxes" a contemporary magazine has this statement:

To expect peace to come only through the passage of legislation is at best ingenuous. "Legislation," the Fellowship underlines, "follows upon changes in attitude, but the changes in attitude are the essential development. Is this kind of activity to be harassed and frustrated? Is . . . the religious and humanitarian conscience of the country . . . [to be limited] to the charity that begins and ends with baskets for the poor?" [2]

The story is told that Clemenceau was commenting with scorn about the visionary plans of Woodrow Wilson following World War I. Clemenceau was interested in revenge upon the Germans for the terrible suffering his nation had undergone. Wilson had other ideas. Finally, in exasperation the French premier is reported to have shouted, "He talks like Jesus Christ!" To which one might comment, "Oh, if he only had!" Peace, reconciliation, the full and abundant life for all involves much more than the manipulation of governments, and far more than the praises of our lips on Palm Sunday.

Albert Schweitzer in his *Philosophy of Civilization* wrote: "The final decision as to what the future of a society shall be depends not on how near its organization is to perfection, but on the degrees of worthiness in its individual members." [3]

III

How shall we answer the question, "Who is this?" in our day? The question should be, "Who am I in relation to him?" We do not measure him in terms of some other standard; he is the standard.

To illustrate: If one were to ask what a pound avoirdupois is, a perfectly correct and accurate answer would be that one pound is .598 percent of me or .00598 of W. T. Viets. But we don't define a pound in that way. If one were to ask what is a foot in measure, a perfectly accurate answer would be that a linear foot is 16.783 percent of W. T. Viets or .16783 of my height. However, we don't define a foot in that way. Rather, the Bureau of Weights and Measures has a series of standards against which all measuring devices are tested. My height and weight are measured against these standards rather than the other way around.

Jesus Christ is now the scale by which I am measured, rather than one whom I define in terms of my desires or understanding. He is the standard against which all else is tested. He "who by the power at work within us is able to do far more abundantly than all we ask or think" (Eph. 3:20).

> He walks among us still, unseen,
> And still points out the only way.[4]

He points out that when men have done their worst against him and when his followers have done their pitiful best for him and then fallen away, then God takes over. This is equally true for the individual, for a society, for a nation.

IV

"Who is this?" "What's going on here?" That is not the question the world must ask. Rather, "Who am I?" "What is our society?" "What is our nation?" What is the relation to one who rode in on the donkey, but who went to a cross, suffered and died in self-sacrificing love, but was not defeated by the cross? We have an empty cross in our churches to remind us that God would not allow him to be defeated by the cross, but carried him to victory after men had done their worst. Who is this? No, who am I in relation to him?

Thanks be to God for the privilege of being numbered among the fellowship of those who strive to be measured by him and to be found worthy in his sight.

7. "Why Do You Seek the Living Among the Dead?"

THE QUESTION OF LIFE

(Easter)
Scripture: Luke 23:50—24:12

"He is risen!"

"He is risen, indeed!"

Even as we echo on the glorious Easter morning the traditional glad exultant shout which has rung down through the ages, we are conscious of a question posed by the angelic messenger which probes beneath our joyous celebration and brings us up short. For often it seems that we seek the living among the dead.

If the characteristic shout for Palm Sunday is "Hosanna" surely the characteristic exclamation for Easter is "Hallelujah" or "Praise the Lord." Even as we sing our praises, however, we recognize that here is mystery. Here is much which we can never completely describe. We will search the Scriptures in vain for a coherent, logical, rational description of exactly what took place and how it took place on that Resurrection morn. We find contradiction of detail in the

Gospel accounts and confusion as to the method. We do well to acknowledge the fact.

But here is great meaning. We acknowledge this and thank God for it. If we search the Scriptures we will discover, to our great profit, the eternal meaning of the fact of the Resurrection and the new vision, new life, that came through it into the lives of those who accepted it and responded to it. Mystery? Yes, but also meaning.

Let us think together about the question asked from the tomb of the women who came seeking him in a graveyard from whence he had gone. We shall reexamine the account of blasted hope as recorded by Luke and compare it with our own. We shall consider the question as posed to the women and see how it applies to us. We shall then rephrase the question in a way which speaks significantly to our day.

I

Rereading the accounts of the events following the crucifixion of Jesus reveals the despair, utter loneliness, and the feeling of having been forsaken of the disciples and all those who had fled from that dead, broken form upon the cross. Their hopes were dead; their glorious dreams were all blasted. It was over—finished!

There was one among the council, who, though he had been powerless to prevent the Crucifixion, yet had been sympathetic to Jesus and so obtained permission from the Roman governor to take the body and give it decent burial. Joseph provided the necessary materials and a newly hewn tomb in which the body was lovingly placed. The tomb was sealed. All then rested on the Sabbath, according to the law. As soon as the first light of dawn appeared on the first day of the week, some women came to the tomb. Did they come because they just could not accept the inevitable? Or did they come for what comfort they might gain from remembering their blasted dreams before the tomb? For whatever reason, they took spices and ointment and went to the tomb, not knowing what they would find, nor how they would roll back the stone. Then they found the tomb empty! There also came the words, "Why do you seek the living among the dead? Remember how he told you, while he was still in Galilee, that the Son of man must be delivered into the hands of sinful men, and be crucified, and on the third day rise." (Luke 24:5-7.) Immediately they rushed back to share it with the others. But the others dismissed it as the idle tale of babbling, hysterical women who, out of their grief or through hallucination, didn't know what they were talking about. At least, this is the way Luke describes it.

Has not each of us gone through similar experiences, even though on a less sublime level? There is not one among us who has not known blasted hopes, has not known despair, has not seen the death of some dream. But after burying it, have we continued to turn it over in memory and imagination, bitterly yearning for that which is gone? Or have we been able to gain new perspective from the experience? To many of us the question from the tomb is directed: Why do *we* seek the living among the dead? Why do *we* seek for meaning and purpose in that which is gone and past?

II

There are many ways in which we, as individuals, and our society are seeking the meaning of life, the purpose and will of God in that which is dead and gone, rather than in resurrection truth, which remains current and vital.

How many persons there are whose lives are empty of meaning and excitement because they spend all their energies either yearning over something that is already gone or for something that has not yet come in the future. There are so many middle-aged people who can't come to terms with middle-age, and there are many teen-agers who can't come to terms with this glorious developing stage but destroy it in yearning to be twenty or thirty. Why do they seek the living reality among the dead years that are gone or the years not yet come to life? So many destroy the present by yearning after the past or longing for the future. The sampler on the wall of a colonial farmhouse reflects wisdom: "Yesterday is dead; leave it. Tomorrow may never come; don't worry. Today is here; live it." We honor and learn from the past, of course, but are not chained to it. We anticipate the future, of course, but not to the extent of destroying the present where we live. "Enjoy the going and stop thinking so fiercely of the getting there!" Unlike the pitiful vacationer who spends so much time and energy bemoaning the fact that his vacation is slipping away that he never gets any enjoyment or recreation from it. "Why seek the living among the dead?"

Does the foregoing sound trivial? Especially for Easter? Then ask yourself if our society is seeking life among the dead. We are suspended between a dying world and a world waiting to be born. In which direction shall we or do we look for life? Shall we or do we seek the living among the dead? The United States will never again be a predominantly rural country. The United States will never again be a predominantly monocultural country. The United States will never again be an isolated country—isolated from the rest of the world. None of us will ever again live in protective insulation from other cultures, races, and religions. Why do we so often seek the living among the dead by trying to turn back the clock? How often we assume that we can have again a world in which mankind can be divided up into neat little culture-tight, or racial-tight or religious-tight compartments. "Why seek ye the living among the dead?"

What a privilege it is to live in a pluralistic society. New Haven, Conn., is one of the few cities in which no religious group represents a clear majority. If you divide the population into four categories: Roman Catholic, Protestant, Jewish, and other or non-religious, no one of these groupings represents a clear majority. If we think in old terms in which society was homogeneous and the standards of one group were superimposed upon the others because there were so few of the others that it didn't really matter, this represents quite a change! There are some who would like to return to this old pattern, but we never shall. However, if we recognize the infinite variety of God's creation and man's response to reflect his glory, then we can see that when Jesus prayed in the upper room, "that they may all be one; even as thou, Father, art in me, and I in Thee"

(John 17:21), he was not talking about conformity on the basis of the least common denominator, but in terms of a unity of spirit, a unity of motivation, a unity of respect and concern for one another. Then we can recognize pluralism as a glorious thing because no group has a monopoly upon all truth nor the capacity to confine all truth in its formulations. Of course, I am convinced that my point of view and attitude toward ultimate questions comes closer to God's purpose than that of some other religions, and I stake my life on that conviction, but I can still learn much from others and gain humility, God willing. Some would reject this dialogue and return to the supremacy of one group. This is impossible. "Why seek ye the living among the dead?"

Jesus made reference to the necessity for putting new wine in new bottles rather than trying to cram it into the old inadequate containers. Putting it in the old wineskins would destroy both the containers and the wine. The vision of the brotherhood of man is meaningless apart from the consciousness of the fatherhood of God. But the meaning of brotherhood in current human experience must evolve new containers and new forms. "Why seek the living among the dead?"

How many persons there are who, in their personal lives, seek for happiness and meaning through possessing things. We live in a time when more people have more things to use and enjoy than ever before in the history of mankind. Are we happier? Have we found meaning? Have the television sets, fast cars, automatic washers, really freed us for relaxed and creative activity? I remember so well the childless couple who came to me for counsel in a former parish.

Their income was at least twice the income on which I was raising four children. They were miserable, in spite of their Cadillac roadster and their second car, together with so much of what money could buy, for they had no purpose. Then there was the man who felt he was doing his duty to God by putting five dollars on the offering plate every Easter, but who, despite his belief that he could handle his own affairs, was spending twenty-five dollars for a half-hour with a psychiatrist every week, as his second marriage was going on the rocks. "Why seek the living among the dead?"

We live in a time when a larger proportion of the gross national products of all the nations of the world is put into implements of "security" than ever before in history. Are we secure? Peace is not balance of terror. Peace involves relationships among persons. It requires recognition of value and potential in all other children of God. It requires brotherhood. "Why seek the living among the dead?"

The angelic question from the tomb burns in our day in innumerable ways.

III

Let us rephrase the question. "How can we allow the living to become real and so escape the death of meaninglessness?" Though there is mystery at the tomb, the meaning is that God is stronger than all else; that good is stronger than evil; that life is stronger than death; that love is stronger than hatred. We may not be able to see how it is all going to come out. We may not be able to describe ultimate results, but this is the audacious, incredible, glorious claim

93

of the Christian gospel. How can we allow this living reality
to take possession of us?

Recall the hymn:

Open my eyes that I may see
Glimpses of truth thou hast for me;
Place in my hands the wonderful key
That shall unclasp, and set me free.

Open my ears that I may hear
Voices of truth thou sendest clear;
And while the wave-notes fall on my ear,
Everything false will disappear.

Open my mouth and let me bear
Gladly the warm truth everywhere;
Open my heart, and let me prepare
Love with thy children thus to share.[1]

It is possible in any situation to find something wrong.
The story is told of the village pessimist who, no matter
what, always found something to complain about. For
several years the crops had been poor. But one year there
was a magnificent harvest. The potatoes were big and
mealy. The townsfolk felt that now, at last, the pessimist
would be unable to complain. Some of them asked him
what he thought of the fine potato crop. Looking around
at the rich harvest, he said, querulously, "But where are
the little ones to feed the pigs?"

Some people can find something wrong in any situation.
Some people can find something good in every situation.

I'm not suggesting a superficial "Pollyannaism," but the longer I am in the Christian ministry, the more amazed I am at the unseen resources upon which some people are able to call in time of stress. Many is the time when after a crisis call, I have felt more ministered to than ministering. There are so many who have discovered for themselves the truth of Paul's statement to the church at Rome: "We know that in everything God works for good with those who love him, who are called after his purpose." (Rom. 8:28.) How do we receive this? By accepting it and responding to it. For this is the meaning of the Resurrection, is it not? Not a dead fact back there almost two thousand years ago, but living reality here and now.

When he was presiding bishop of the Protestant Episcopal Church, Arthur Lichtenberger distributed an annual Easter message. One of these read, in part:

Through his life and death and resurrection, Christ has opened for us the gate of everlasting life which means that he has opened up new possibilities of life now. But a gate leads no-where for us unless we walk through it. The fact of Christ means nothing in our lives unless we . . . respond to it. Easter then, when we celebrate it as Christian people, is a festival as wide as all creation and as personal as my own thoughts and desires. What God did in Jesus Christ he did for the whole created order; he was reconciling the *world* to himself. Here is the focus and center of all our attention: "Maker and Redeemer, life and health of all." But then I realize this was for me, that Christ lived and died and rose again to open up new possibilities of life for me. And so the only response that has any meaning is my own personal commitment of faith: "My

Lord and my God." This is the way out of self-centeredness and the narrow and constricted way that leads to death. This is the way that turns us from ourselves toward the world. This is the way that leads to eternal life *now!*

How to find the living? Accept the gift. The mystery remains. There is mystery all about me. I know that, by some mysterious process a substance known as chlorophyll in the leaves of plants is able to take sunlight and certain elements and transform them into food which I can eat. I don't understand the mystery of the process, but I'm thankful for the nourishment of the food! The mystery remains, but the meaning is there as well. Accept it; appreciate it; respond to it.

With the response comes freedom—freedom from fear. For truly, for so many constant fear, anxiety, and uncertainty are death in life. John Sutherland Bonnell has described it like this:

A Roman magistrate greets a Christian prisoner, standing in the dock, with these words: "I sentence you to death as a follower of the Nazarene." But the prisoner looks unflinchingly into the eyes of the magistrate and replies, "Sir, death is dead. It no longer has power to make me afraid. Our divine Master has conquered death and the grave. He said to us, 'Be not afraid of them that kill the body, and after that have no more that they can do.'"

So Rome lost the one instrument by which it had hoped to put fear into the hearts of these Christians. Little wonder that within three hundred years the cross of the despised Galilean took precedence over the Roman eagle.

To this day the most convincing evidence for the resurrection of Christ is men and women whose lives bear witness to his living reality.²

The poet:

>We call this Time, and gauge it by the clock,
>   Deep in such insect cares as suit that view:—
>   As whether dresses fit, what modes are new,
>And where to buy, and when to barter, stock.
>We think we hold, based on some Scripture rock,
>   Claims on immortal life, to press when due:
>   Imagining some door between the two,
>Our deaths shall each, with presto change! unlock.
>
>But this is also everlasting life!
>   On Monday, in the kitchen, street, or store,
>We are immortal, we, the man and wife;
>   Immortal now, or shall be nevermore.
>Immortals in immortal values spend
>Those lives that shall no more begin than end.³

Many have read William Ernest Henley's "Invictus" and thrilled at its courage but been appalled by its shallowness. A Christian layman, responding to that self-centered prideful poem, wrote:

>Out of the fathomless womb of Time,
>   Fashioned by Love at God's decree,
>I came to earth, a soul, to climb
>   Back to my heavenly destiny.
>
>Equipped by mind and heart divine;
>   Clothed in a form by God designed,
>I hold The Master's power in mine
>   To be and do as He assigned.

My upward path by sin, I know,
  Will be beset; but this I claim;
I shall be conqueror and go
  Forever forward in His name!

It matters not how soon or late
  He orders closed my earthly scroll;
With Him I'm Master of My Fate!
  Through Him I'm Captain of my soul![4]

So often it is through poetry that mystery is acknowledged and meaning communicated.

IV

We began our thought together with the glad affirmation "He is risen!" We face the mystery of the Resurrection and accept its meaning with humble gratitude. We conclude with the affirmation, recasting our question, that God in Christ can and will rescue us from seeking life among death and lead us into life abundant, here and beyond. Thanks be to him for his wondrous gift, so wondrously given!

Epilogue
"Do You Love Me More Than These?"

THE CONTINUING QUESTION

(The Sunday After Easter)
Scripture: John 21:1-25

"How great is your love? Do you love me more than these others love me? Do you love me more than you love these other things?"

Traditionally through much of Judeo-Christian history the octave of a festival, that is the week following the festival, has been celebrated as part of the festival. This seems particularly significant with Easter, for though Easter as the Festival of the Resurrection may be the climax of the gospel story, it is not the end. Indeed, its meaning carries over to the Sunday and the Sundays beyond the Easter experience itself, else its meaning is lost. Actually, we celebrate the first day of the week as holy day instead of the seventh as a weekly reminder of the Resurrection. Furthermore, we can be certain that the congregation on the Sunday after Easter will be composed of the committed core of the Christian fellowship and possibly a few who have been par-

99

ticularly influence by the Lenten-Easter period. It will be a more intimate fellowship than that of the preceding Sunday. The question posed at the start is one that was asked by Christ in an intimate setting.

If you had been forsaken by a group of close friends in your hour of trial, how would you greet them the next time you saw them? If you were one who had forsaken a friend in time of need, how would you expect to be greeted? These considerations add dimension to the question.

I

Apparently the question was asked of Peter. But it has implications for all the disciples and, by extension, for us as well. Earlier in the passion narrative Jesus had predicted that the disciples would fall away. It was Peter who spoke up and proclaimed his steadfastness. And it was Peter who denied Jesus three times. The writer of the Fourth Gospel, perhaps out of concern for internal literary structure, directs in this appendix chapter the three questions to Peter, thus balancing the denials. The Synoptic accounts indicate that not only Peter proclaimed steadfastness. In Matthew after Peter had said, "Even if I must die with you, I will not deny you," the next sentence reads: "And so said all the disciples." (26:25.) Consequently, though the writer of the Fourth Gospel directs the question at Peter in this post-Resurrection episode, we can assume the question is directed at all of the rest of us who may be tempted to claim, "Yes, I'm strong enough," but who find out that alone we are not. Perhaps we, too, can go through the

100

rest of the experience and discover that there is strength not our own, beyond anything we dreamed before.

Let us now reconstruct the scene; consider the question itself, thrice repeated in slightly different form; examine the meaning of the commission of Christ and give thought to the sequel.

II

With all the post-Resurrection appearances of Christ, we are aware that accurate, detailed physical and material description is impossible. Each has a message to communicate. This one shows the disciples attempting to pick up the thread of their ordinary lives again. They have returned to the familiar surroundings of home in Galilee. After the overwhelming experiences of the life with Jesus, the blighting of their hopes and the joy of the Resurrection, they sought emotional equilibrium again by returning to that which they had known before. Peter's comment, "I'm going fishing" was not an indication that he was going off on a vacation, but that he was returning to his familiar occupation. He was really saying, "I'm going to try to pick up the broken threads of my life. I'm after emotional and also economic security." So said they all. There is value in this attitude. Sorrow is but the rust of the soul; activity will cleanse and brighten it. Often a return to the routine is a person's salvation.

We will not comment at any length on the miraculous draft of fishes described in the account. Some scholars claim this is not germane to the passage. It may be that, after fishing all night and catching nothing, as dawn was breaking they profited from the fact that Christ, standing high above them on the bank, was able to see in the clear waters of the lake, a school of fish they had overlooked. Nor are we interested in the myriad allegorical interpretations derived from the number of fish involved! None of these speculations add anything to the point of the story as we see it. They went fishing; Christ appeared to them; Peter, in his usual enthusiasm, when he realized who it was, couldn't wait for the boat to come to shore, but leaped overboard and waded in. Christ had kindled a fire and prepared their breakfast. Perhaps there is symbolic significance in the meal, but we'll not pause on that, either. Our interest centers on the spirit of Christ and the questions.

Note, first, one very important thing. There is no word of recrimination from the lips of the Master. He did not say to them, "So, you thought you were strong enough! You thought you could stand firm!" No, there is nothing of this from him. However, it is necessary to reestablish the relationship of commitment. After the meal, therefore, the question is asked of Peter first, but by implication of all of them and by extension of us as well.

"Do you love me more than these?" What does "more than these" mean? Scholars differ as to whether it means, "Do you love me more than these others love me?" or "Do you love me more than you love these other things?" Perhaps both are implied. Both have significance, though the first suggests a competitive relationship between the disciples that seems out of character for Christ. He had previously rebuked similar statements by the disciples

themselves. The second alternative seems more significant—
"Do you love me more than you love these other things?"
Do you love me more than you love the security, the
familiarity, the return to the routine of everyday life? At
least that's the way the question comes to us.

III

Scholars disagree as to the importance of the fact that in
the version we have, two different verbs are used for the
question dealing with love. In the first two instances, in
the Greek, the verb used emphasizes considered commitment or intellectual understanding. Peter answers in each
case with a verb that involves emotional attachment and
reaction from the heart. We might paraphrase the exchange
like this:

"Are you committed to me, Peter?"

To which Peter answered, "I am your friend."

A second time: "Are you committed to me, Peter?"

"Well, I'm your friend!"

"Are you my friend?"

"You know everything, Lord." (By implication, "I've been
wrong before.") "I think I'm your friend, but you know
everything; you know whether or not I am." Surrender, sub-
mission, commitment.

Placing the questions and answers this way indicates that
Christian commitment involves both the head and the heart
—both understanding and realization—both knowing and
trusting beyond knowledge. It was Francis Bacon who
pointed out with amazement that Aristotle, in all of his
writings about ethics, never says anything about the af-

fections and the emotions. Yet, ethical choice and moral decision can never be entirely objective and abstract, academic and intellectual. Emotional commitment which transforms faith from mere belief to trust is essential. Full commitment—full response to God in Christ—requires both head and heart. Either without the other can lead to unhappy results. On the one hand, there is the wise person who prayed, "O Lord, forgive us for being enthusiastically wrong!" Emotion without understanding. On the other hand there is T. S. Eliot's

> The last temptation is the greatest treason:
> To do the right deed for the wrong reason.[1]

Understanding without emotion. It is not "either or," but "both and."

IV

Each of the Gospel accounts has some form of the great commission left by Christ to his followers. John includes his version in the three comments made by Jesus after the three questions and response. Once again, since they seem to be divided, we shall leave to the scholars the question of the significance of the fact that different verbs are used. Continuing our paraphrase begun earlier, it seems that Christ is saying, "If you are intellectually committed, and if you are emotionally attached, then certain things will follow." There are three of these, which together describe pretty completely, the privilege and opportunity of the Christian fellowship which is the church: Feed lambs; tend sheep; feed sheep.

We do feed the lambs about us. We do communicate values and moral standards to the young, whether we know it or not. Are we giving Christian understanding by example? Are we instilling Christian motivations and high moral standards by the lives we live?

A horrible story came to my attention recently. A beautiful, young high school senior girl, caught up on the clouds with her approaching graduation and all the round of parties and festivities, set out for the senior prom with a fine young classmate. Later that night her parents received a phone call from the state police. At the scene of the accident the father looked down on the lifeless mangled body of his daughter. As they examined the car, they found a whiskey bottle in the car. In his anguish the father vowed, "If I ever get my hands on the guy who gave them that bottle, I'll kill him!" When the father returned home, feeling the need of something to bolster himself, he went to his liquor closet. There was a bottle missing. In its place was a note signed by his daughter which read, "Daddy, we borrowed your bottle tonight, because we knew you would want us to have a good time."

"Feed my lambs." You do feed my lambs. What moral standards are you giving them? There is a sign on the Connecticut turnpike which reads, "Would you teach your child to drive that way?" "Feed my lambs."

Christian freedom is not the freedom to indulge oneself and then justify and rationalize that self-indulgence. Christian freedom is freedom from the necessity for self-indulgence and the freedom to be the kind of witness that will make a positive impression. For the power of example

105

works in that direction, too. Thanks be to God for it. How many lives have been influenced for good by the example of other upstanding persons, usually unconscious of their influence. "If you love me, you will feed my lambs."

"If you love me, you will tend my sheep." Carl Jung in *Modern Man in Search of a Soul* suggests that in the middle years, about forty, a subtle change comes into the lives of most persons. No longer is there the expectancy of youth but the necessity to learn to live with what is and the knowledge that it's not going to change a great deal. When children are no longer dependent upon their parents, this change begins. Other factors also enter in. Some, in the face of the change, live the rest of their lives in quiet desperation. Others face the new conditions creatively. But all need the bolstering and sustaining fellowship of friendly concern and support. Those who truly love will tend the sheep and help provide this support. The pastoral function in the Christian fellowship is not something which is provided only by the clergyman. It is an enterprise of the whole "concerned community," which is but another name for the church. This pastoral privilege cannot be carried out just by the professional leaders. It is a cooperative task of the whole fellowship. The early Methodist class meetings and the prayer and study fellowships and various cell groups and neighborhood zone programs of more modern Protestantism are carrying this out. Thanks be to God for the privilege. "If you love me, you will tend to the needs of one another."

"If you love me, you will feed my sheep." There is none among us who would expect to go into a computer laboratory and run one of the great electronic brains using the arithmetic we had learned by the time we joined the church as young people. But how many there are, in the face of changing conditions and the chaotic and confusing situations in which we find ourselves now, who are trying to face this world on the basis of what was learned religiously by the eighth grade! "If you are committed to me both intellectually and emotionally, you will recognize as a fellowship the tremendous opportunity to raise up the great moral questions of the day and to bring the eternal relevance of the Incarnation to bear upon them."

Everett W. Palmer wrote: "When followers of Jesus Christ . . . are not being slandered or persecuted, one of two things is true: Either they have Christianized the world or the world has paganized them!" Raise the great questions, knowing that truth does not change, but the application of truth changes. An economics professor was called upon by a student with a troubled conscience. The student had discovered that the final examination in one course was the same year after year. After discovering this, he went to the professor and told him what he had found out. He was certain others knew this as well, and this didn't seem right. But the professor was undisturbed, for, said he, "That's perfectly all right. We ask the same questions every year, but, you see, in economics, we change the answers!" This is not intended to be just a snide comment on the inexactness of economic theory, but to indicate that conditions do change and that we must keep our minds open to new understanding.

During World War II there were two shopkeepers in

London who were great rivals. During the bombings each made a great point of being open for business every morning, even though his store may have been damaged the night before. One night, however, the attack was so devastating that the whole front of one of the shops was completely gone. This shopkeeper's competitor, however, though damaged, had a large sign on the front of his shop which read, "Open as usual." What to do? Our friend could not be outdone by his competitor. So he took a large piece of cardboard and lettered a sign which read, "More open than usual!" This says something to the church. We need to be more open than usual to the changing currents of thought, the changing questions of moral value, the changing needs of people. The sheep, as well as the lambs, need to be fed.

"If you love me, you will feed my lambs; you will tend my sheep; you will feed my sheep."

V

Consider now the sequel to all this. After talking with Christ, Peter asked him what was to happen to one of the other disciples. Christ, gently, but firmly, said, in effect, "That's really none of your business." "It is no concern of yours what my purposes are for him." So often we wish to compare ourselves with others and wish to compare them and their accomplishments with us and ours. Sometimes it seems as though there is little correspondence between the zeal and devotion of some people and the level of life that they live. But that's not in my hands. Each person's responsibility is simply to discover God's commission for him (or her) and to leave the results with God. I am not called upon to judge my brother. I am only called upon to follow Christ out of gratitude.

When Robert Morrison went out to China as the first Christian missionary to that country in 1807, a prosperous businessman is reputed to have approached him on the ship with the scornful question, "Do you really think you are going to have any effect upon the idolatry of the Chinese empire?" To which Morrison quietly replied, "No, but I expect that God will."

Christ asks us all, not only during the Lenten-Easter period, but constantly, "Do you love me?" Then he says, in effect, "If you do, then, through you, I shall feed my lambs, tend my sheep, and feed my sheep."

Thanks be to God for the privilege of being his agents.

Chapter 1

1. Samuel Butler, "Hudibras," Part I, Canto I, line 215.
2. (New York: Harper & Brothers, 1943), pp. 21-22.
3. Copyright 1952 Christian Century Foundation. Reprinted by permission from the February 6, 1952, issue of *The Christian Century*.
4. (New York: Friendship Press, 1938).
5. "Christians Who Unwittingly Play the Communist Game," *United Church Herald*, November 29, 1962, p. 10.
6. The author accepts conclusions in *The Interpreter's Bible*, VIII, 460-61, and elsewhere that John 14 belongs after John 15 and 16.

Chapter 2

1. (New York: Oxford University Press, 1950), p. vii.
2. *Yale News and Review*, February 21, 1963, p. 4.
3. *Newsweek*, January 7, 1963, p. 36.
4. Sidney Moss and Samuel Moss, *Thy Men Shall Fall* (New York: Ziff-Davis Publishing Co., 1948).
5. *War and Civilization*, p. 130.
6. Quoted by permission of writer.

111

Chapter 3

1. William C. Bryant, "The Battle-Field."
2. John Keats, "Ode on a Grecian Urn."
3. "The Present Crisis."
4. Reprinted by permission of Virgil Markham.

Chapter 4

1. *The Interpreter's Bible* (Nashville: Abingdon Press, 1951), VII, 897-98.
2. "Indifference."
3. Frederick Faber, "There's a Wideness in God's Mercy."
4. "The Great Wager." Used by permission of Harper & Row and Hodder & Stoughton Ltd.
5. Shakespeare, *Merchant of Venice*, Act V, Scene I.
6. Elizabeth Cheney, "There Is a Man on the Cross."

Chapter 5

1. Author unknown.
2. Pp. lxxvii f.
3. *Guide to Understanding the Bible* (New York: Harper & Row, 1938), p. 193.

Chapter 6

1. *The Christian Century*, March 20, 1963, p. 357.
2. *The Village Voice*, March, 1963.
3. (New York: The Macmillan Company, 1950), p. 45.
4. John Oxenham, "He—They—We." Used by permission of Theo Oxenham.

Chapter 7

1. Clara H. Scott.
2. *Heaven and Hell* (Nashville: Abingdon Press, 1956), pp. 60-61.
3. Sarah N. Cleghorn, "But This Is Also Everlasting Life."
4. "Victor Through Him," Frederick Abbott.

Epilogue

1. *Murder in the Cathedral*. Used by permission of Harcourt, Brace & World and Faber and Faber Ltd.